Mid-Atlantic National Parks
FIVE TOUR GUIDEBOOK
By Michael Frome

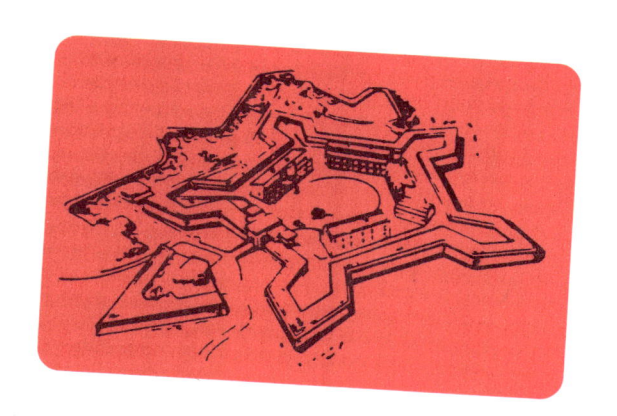

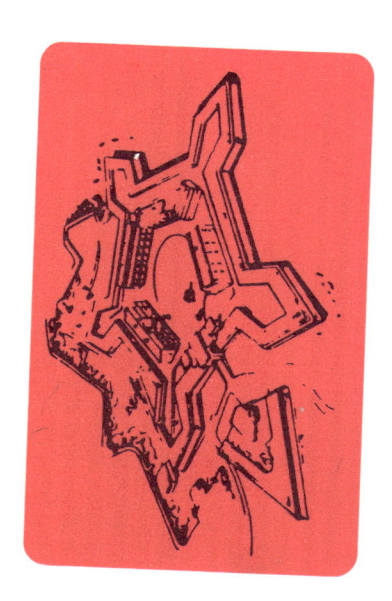

Tour of Colonial and Revolutionary Times
Tour of Rivers and Wild Nature
Tour of Industry and Engineering
Tour of Civil War Scenes
Great Americans Tour

In grateful
remembrance to
DOROTHY W. HAAS

Charter member of the National Parks Mid-Atlantic Council having served from its inception in 1982-1986, Dophie is affectionately remembered with greatest admiration and respect for her dedicated service.

1986

COPYRIGHT© *1987 By The National Parks Mid-Atlantic Council*

Manufactured in The United States of America

INTRODUCTION

In 1872, Congress established Yellowstone as "a public park or pleasuring-ground for the benefit and enjoyment of the people." Few, if any, of the legislators who favored setting aside Yellowstone could have realized the kind of impact its creation would ultimately play. Yellowstone was the first of its kind. The idea of a "national park" was an invention created from American experience, prudence, and ingenuity. Although no plan initially existed to build a "system" of such parks, Yellowstone has since come to represent the philosophical beginning of what has now become known as the National Park System.

Today, the National Park System encompasses areas from the Atlantic Coast of Maine to Guam and Saipan in the distant Pacific, and from far north of the Arctic Circle in Alaska to the Virgin Islands in the sub-tropical Caribbean. The System currently embraces over 300 units all set aside to be managed by the National Park Service consistent with its obligation "to conserve the scenery and the natural and historic objects and the wild life therein and to provide for the enjoyment of the same...in such manner and by such means as will leave them unimpaired for the enjoyment of future generations."

Americans have provided for conservation of cultural and natural resources in National Park System areas. Through these areas, Americans have been afforded access to places and experiences otherwise unattainable where they can go to relax, do some reflecting, and generally enjoy themselves. However, that's not all these areas offer! They also offer the public areas to explore, study, and learn about this great nation of ours. Thus,

National Park system areas have proven to be more than "just a place to go to," they are a vital part of our heritage that must be preserved not only for us today, but also for those who follow.

Conserving these unique areas—each made up of complex mixtures of values and resources—while also providing for the enjoyment of some 400 million visitors yearly has been no easy task. But we have not carried this responsibility alone. We owe much to volunteers. Time and again, the Service has been assisted by conscientious volunteers anxious to freely put forth their time, talent, and support. There have been so many instances of volunteers coming to our aid, I cannot even begin to acknowledge them all. I can, however, say that each volunteer has been greatly appreciated.

This publication is a good example of the kinds of contributions volunteers can make. The publication of this guidebook was made possible by the National Parks Mid-Atlantic Regional Council, an alliance of local volunteers and citizen groups initially fostered by the National Parks and Conservation Association, to exercise responsibility and turn concern for specific national parks in their areas into action. I congratulate the Mid-Atlantic Council on its good work and the author, Michael Frome, on his contribution. This guidebook will surely be a great source of information to visitors for many years to come.

William Penn Mott, Jr.
Director, National Park Service

ACKNOWLEDGEMENTS

National parks preserve and interpret the finest of nature and of our past. They offer knowledge, but not simply the kind that come from books. More like a living library, national parks make it possible to be on the scene itself—standing in the room where a great event transpired, walking in the pathways of native Americans and pioneer settlers through a centuries-old forest, floating on a sparkling river that still runs free.

National parks combine education with inspiration and recreation. For 30 years I've been describing their special features and showing readers how best to enjoy them. It's been a labor of love, since I have never visited a national park I didn't like, where I didn't yearn to stay longer or to revisit.

I feel privileged at having the opportunity to prepare this manuscript. I acknowledge with appreciation the constructive leadership of Mary C. Carroll, chair of the National Parks Mid-Atlantic Regional Council, and the cooperation of Council members. I appreciate the encouragement of James W. Coleman, Jr., Director of the Mid-Atlantic Region of the National Park Service; Chester O. Harris, Chief, Interpretation and Visitor Services of the Mid-Atlantic Region; and park superintendents, rangers and interpreters in the various parks. I know that I speak for all concerned in expressing gratitude to the William Penn Foundation, of Philadelphia, for the grant that has made this publication possible.

Visiting a national park, any national park, is a rewarding experience. It can be stimulating and challenging, sparking the visitor to examine his or her community for challenges and opportunities. There may not be a point in saving anything and everything merely because it is old or wild. But every town, city, and county needs to have its own choice spots while there is still time.

The thoughtful, creative national parks traveler can bring that message home and put it to work. Protecting open spaces and stone and brick symbols of our civilization enriches the environment and the quality of life.

Michael Frome
Northland College
Ashland, Wisconsin

CONTENTS

Introduction 3
How to Use This Guidebook 9
Tour of Colonial and Revolutionary Times 13
Tour of Rivers and Wild Nature 43
Tour of Industry and Engineering 73
Tour of Civil War Scenes 89
Great Americans Tour 115

HOW TO USE THIS GUIDEBOOK

With this book as your guide, you can plan your travels to national parks in the Mid-Atlantic States of New Jersey, Pennsylvania, Maryland, Virginia and West Virginia. These parks tell many stories of nature and history, and of the people who played roles in shaping the country we know today.

The concept of this guidebook is that visiting individual national parks randomly, though rewarding, gives only a piecemeal picture, a fractured understanding of individual park stories. On the other hand, to visit within a given time frame a sequence of parks all relating to the same theme will provide a more comprehensive and satisfying experience. Each tour has been outlined as an adventure in learning for all ages. Because each tour takes at least a weekend, it could be considered an enjoyable family vacation as well.

Five tours are outlined in the following chapters. Each tour attempts to proceed chronologically. You will find it helpful to refer to the map just inside the cover, since it identifies all the parks and major sites on the tours.

Additionally, the map at the beginning of each chapter pinpoints parks which are part of that chapter theme tour. Other parks nearby relating to different themes and various points of interest are also included.

I advise use of this guidebook in conjunction with a good road map and other references. There are suggested routes to follow, in some cases, but feel free to start anywhere. It's often a good idea to get off the interstates and travel the back roads. Go slower and enjoy it more.

Restaurants, hotel accommodations, and other tourist facilities are mentioned here and there as a service to the guidebook user. However, these are only recommendations from Council members, not recommendations by the National Park Service.

National parks give us many insights into our country. This leads me to mention a special way to appreciate and enjoy national parks. Let's call it the unhurried approach. It begins with pre-trip planning: investing energy in advance to estimate distances, times enroute, a budget of expenses, and an idea of overnight lodgings. Pre-trip planning should also include reading about your chosen points of interest. I strongly suggest using the boxed information at the end of each stop on the tour. Drop a letter to the park to request information to be sent to you before your trip. You'll be glad you did, for this advance effort will enable you to see and absorb more while traveling.

Allow plenty of time when you arrive at a park, going first to the park visitor center. Here, there will be a park ranger on duty, exhibit displays, and introductory audio-visual programs. Inquire about the schedule of guided walks and talks, campfire programs, demonstrations and other activities, and pick up maps and literature for further guidance. Make it a point to speak with one of the rangers. These men and women are there to assist you and to protect park resources.

A slower pace expands the dimensions of time. Get off the main trails into quiet corners for intimate observation and contemplation in harmony with the setting. The parks have proven their value many times over as sanctuaries of nature, but they are sanctuaries *for* humans as well, affording respite from sights, sounds, smells and pressures of a technological civilization. The historical parks feature some of the finest architecture in America. Make the most of it by examining the distinctive features, and the patterns and texture of brick, stone and wood that reveal the inherent character and individuality of each structure.

Prepare to find nature and history as partners in the field. You may go to Gettysburg to view the Civil War battle scene, but you will also be treated to a rich variety and abundance of birds, including vultures soaring on the wind currents. At Jamestown, keep your eye peeled for deer. Natural area parks often embrace fascinating cultural aspects, such as the displays of mountaineer life at Shenandoah National Park. Be open and alert to discoveries and surprises—they add to understanding and appreciation.

The parks of Washington, D.C., are not covered in this guidebook. That would take a volume in itself. The National Park Service administers all major monuments and memorials (including those to Washington, Jefferson and Lincoln) and nearly everything green in the city, from the Mall to Rock Creek Park and Civil War fortifications that once protected the capital. Consider Washington for a separate excursion. When you do go there, be sure to Dial-A-Park (202/426-6975) or the National Capital Region (202/426-6700) to ask about special events, entry fees (where they may apply), and opening and closing hours at the parks.

Of course, national parks are governed by rules and regulations. They need to be, considering the heavy volume of visitors they receive and the importance of protecting their resources. These rules involve simple courtesy and common sense; therefore, you will find here no "do's" and "don'ts." If you have questions or feel unsure, speak to a ranger or see if the park has prepared special literature. Otherwise, consider that appreciation of the resource and good common sense will promote safety and reduce the impact of visitors.

Your dog or cat is welcome, but keep it on a leash, in your car, or caged. Remember not to leave a pet in the car on a hot day—it may suffer heat stroke, even with the windows open. Pets are not permitted in public buildings, on trails or in designated areas at specific parks. This is particularly important at Assateague Island National Seashore, where pets are prohibited both in the state park and the Chincoteague National Wildlife Refuge.

The best "rule" is not a rule at all, but the idea that parents should set an example for their children. Once I watched a young boy carving his name on a stone monument as his father watched nearby. I commented on the act to his father. "But lots of others have already carved their names," his father retorted a little sheepishly. Hopefully, he got the point. I can't think of a better place than national parks to encourage pride in America and good citizenship. The simplest lesson is learning respect for the physical presence that meets your eyes.

To further enhance your trip along the pathways of America's heritage, the National Parks Passport program was initiated as a guide. You may purchase the Passport and annual national and regional stamps, which depict our nation's natural and cultural heritage, at participating park sites—some of which are in the Mid-Atlantic Region. Each park has a cancellation stamp, allowing you to record each visit on your journey to the past. Proceeds will be used to benefit the preservation and operation of our National Park System, in building a stronger foundation for the future of America's National Parks.

Visit the national parks as the great preserves of yesterday, today and tomorrow and feel that you, too, are in harmony with something special, enriched by the experience, yet leaving the physical places as a gift to others who will follow you.

Tour One

1. Jamestown National Historic Site
2. Colonial Parkway
3. Yorktown Battlefield at Colonial National Historical Park
4. Cape Henry Memorial (Ft. Story Military Reservation)
5. Ft. McHenry National Monument and Historic Shrine
6. Valley Forge National Historical Park
7. Morristown National Historical Park
8. Ft. Necessity National Battlefield
9. Independence National Historical Park

Additional Sights

(A) George Washington Birthplace National Monument
(B) Mount Vernon
(C) Fredericksburg National Military Park
(D) Hampton National Historic Site
(E) Washington Crossing State Park
(F) Hopewell Furnace National Historic Site
(G) Friendship Hill National Historical Park
(H) Fallingwater

Tour One

The Heart of Early History
A Tour of Colonial and Revolutionary Times

On May 13, 1607, three small ships moored on the shore of the James River after five perilous months at sea. The travelers rejoiced; they determined to call their new home Jamestown and thus made it the first permanent settlement of English-speaking people in the New World. Here, in Tidewater Virginia, English traditions were transplanted from one continent to another and representative government in America began.

Why did they come? What problems did the settlers face in clearing the land, building homes, obtaining food, getting along with the natives they encountered, and with each other? How, from this beginning, did colonization advance and lead ultimately to the emergence of a new nation?

This tour provides the opportunity to learn the answers at major landmarks where early American history was written. The logical starting point is 17th century Jamestown. The closest national park unit to it (geographically if not chronologically), Colonial National Historical Park at Yorktown, commemorates the site where the British surrender led to the end of the American Revolution. These two areas are within 23 miles of each other, joined by the Colonial Parkway, one of the finest scenic drives in America. And midway between them, Colonial Williamsburg saw the flowering of culture and public institutions. It belongs on any tour of early American history.

The Heart of Early History

From Tidewater Virginia the tour leads north, within reach of national park units covered in other sections of this guide. With little digression, you can stop at Civil War battlefield parks, George Washington Birthplace National Monument, and Washington's home at Mount Vernon.

Fort McHenry National Monument and Historic Shrine, three miles from the center of Baltimore, is still another important and appealing point of interest. While primarily remembered as the site of the writing of "The Star Spangled Banner," it reflects early efforts of the young republic to achieve recognition in the family of nations.

Twenty miles west of Philadelphia, Valley Forge National Historical Park conveys the sense of suffering and sacrifice endured by common soldiers during the Revolution. If you're coming from the north, be sure to stop at Morristown National Historical Park, in New Jersey, where Washington reorganized his weary forces almost in sight of British lines in New York. And if coming from the west, don't miss Fort Necessity National Battlefield (about an hour's drive southeast of Pittsburgh, near Uniontown), one of the hidden gems of the National Park Service, the site of George Washington's first military engagement in 1754. Or stop at Hopewell Furnace National Historical Park near Elverson, not far from Reading, PA. It's the finest surviving example of many charcoal ironworks that sparked development in eastern America.

From whatever direction, the tour reaches its climax at Independence National Historical Park, where Congress, after the bitter, trying days of the Revolution, adopted the Declaration of Independence and the Constitution. Independence Hall is the focal point but in block after block you can see and explore historic and architectural monuments that figured in the birth of the nation.

Colonial National Historical Park
Jamestown—A Place for Imagination

From the approach causeway on the Colonial Parkway, the unfolding view of the James River embraces ferries crossing between the two shores and freighters traveling upstream and down. Yet picture the scene as it may have been when the first settlers arrived. Likely they celebrated after the stormy crossing, with hopes and dreams, perhaps fears as well, of making their way in a land that looked as God had made it. For 13 years theirs would be the lone English toe hold along the Atlantic seaboard.

Make your first stop the visitor center to begin the walking tour and to see the film and the displays on Jamestown life, including pewter, iron, firearms, rings, clay pipes, bottles, scissors and ceramics—remarkable pieces that help explain how the settlers lived and worked.

Then walk through the excavated "New Towne." Conjectural paintings above the foundations depict the 17th century buildings as they may have looked. At the west end of the town site, the Old Church tower, the only standing ruin of the 17th century town, was part of the fourth church built on the site. However, the Memorial Church (of 1907) directly behind embraces the cobblestone foundation of an earlier church where the first legislative assembly met in 1619. Also at the west end of the site, known as "Old Towne," a potter produces a variety of articles patterned after 17th century pieces used at Jamestown.

From this setting on the banks of the James, officials and lawmakers governed the colony and promoted the spread of settlement. Such was the undoing of Jamestown. Hampered by its low, swampy environment, the town declined and ultimately was abandoned. Its story, fortunately, has not been lost. The Memorial Cross marks the graves of settlers who probably died during the "starving tyme" (1609-10), when the population

The Old Church Tower is the only remaining 17th century structure still standing at Jamestown, one of the places American history began.

15

The Heart of Early History

This bronze Pocahontas stands near the site where she was married to John Rolfe, an Englishman.

dropped from 500 to less than 60. The nearby statues of Pocahontas and Captain John Smith, overlooking the river, recall two of the principal players who in themselves have become legend.

Leaving the town site, the footbridge over the Pitch and Tar Swamp provides a platform from which to observe and photograph plants and birds of this marshy island. Then stop at the Glasshouse of 1608 (a mile from the visitor center, near the entrance station), a reconstruction, fashioned of hand-hewn beams, of what may have been the country's first "factory." The colonists failed in their dream of a livelihood from glassmaking, but they found something else far more profitable. That, of course, was tobacco, which they planted along the streets, "and all other spare places." Today at the Glasshouse, craftsmen in 17th century dress show how glass was blown in the colonial style. Incidentally, they offer attractive pieces for sale at reasonable prices.

Before departing from Jamestown, consider for a moment the saving of this historic place. In 1893, a citizen group, the Association for the Preservation of Virginia Antiquities (APVA), acquired 23 acres. The remainder of the 1500-acre island became part of Colonial National Historical Park in 1934 and since 1940 Jamestown has been jointly administered by the National Park Service and the APVA. Now, as you leave the island, on the left, just beyond the entrance station, Jamestown Festival Park includes replicas of the Jamestown fort, an Indian long house, and those three small ships—

Susan Constant, Godspeed and *Discovery*—the largest of them only 100 tons. This area, administered by the Jamestown-Yorktown Foundation for the Commonwealth of Virginia, should not be confused with the national park.

In Jamestown's reconstructed Glasshouse, craftsmen demonstrate the art of 17th century glass blowing.

The Parkway to Yorktown

The Colonial Parkway, from Jamestown through Williamsburg to Yorktown, is a special place in itself. It skirts the James River, then the York River, crossing historic creeks, marshes and wetlands. The favored season is spring, when pink and white dogwoods and redbuds landscape the route, but for those with perception and patience every season has its own appeal. Take advantage of turnouts and overlooks to enjoy the riverscapes and sites of early plantations, such as Ringfield and Bellefield.

Yorktown, at the eastern end of the parkway, is still an active community. Several outstanding buildings recall the era when it was a thriving commercial center of perhaps 300 houses, as well as three churches, many inns and ordinaries. Today's visitor can sense the flavor of the past at buildings like Grace Church, built of native marl, and the reconstructed Swan Tavern,

The Heart of Early History

Explore the "James Cittie" site at the western end of the Colonial Parkway, located on the Virginia Penninsula between the James and York rivers.

once a gathering place for colonial merchants and planters and now a noteworthy antique shop.

The two most significant houses in or near Yorktown, however, are the Moore House (on the tour road in the battlefield), where the terms of surrender were negotiated in 1781, completely restored and furnished to its 18th century appearance; and the Nelson House, home of Thomas Nelson, Jr., governor of Virginia and signer of the Declaration of Independence. The Moore House is open for living history tours during the summer. At the Nelson House (located in Yorktown), note the cannonball embedded between the gabled windows. And near the east end of Main Street, be sure to see the Victory Monument, a reflection of the gilded age of the 1880's, when such elaborate ornamentation was in vogue.

Yorktown Battlefield

The visitor center and the museum displays will impart the sense of place and purpose through its film and daily walking tour. In the early autumn days of 1781, Americans and the soldiers and sailors of France fought the last important conflict of the war for independence. The exhibits are thoroughly absorbing, worthy of the history they interpret. They include military tents used by General Washington during the campaign, a walk-through portion of a reconstructed British frigate, and dioramas of the scene, with the audio narrative of a teenager who served as a Continental soldier.

From the observation deck the entire field of action comes into view. Americans and their French allies had advanced from three directions: Admiral De Grasse by sea to effect a naval blockade of the Chesapeake Bay,

Lafayette from the west, and Washington and Rochambeau from the north. The land forces met at Williamsburg and drove ahead from there.

Take a self-guiding auto tour of the battlefield. The two focal points are Redoubt 9, taken in heroic action by French infantry and Redoubt 10, captured by the Americans. But many markers and field displays explain the action, and all of the reconstructed earthworks are priceless treasures. Besides the historic values, the entire Tour Road offers scenic and natural vistas. Wormley Pond is especially striking in autumn with the changing colors. The areas around Washington's headquarters, the French Artillery Park, and the French Encampment are well suited to photography or merely reflection on the happenings here.

Surrender Field undoubtedly is one of the most significant spots in American history, for here the British marched out from Yorktown to lay

Walk through part of a reconstructed British frigate and see objects recovered from the York River in the Yorktown Visitor Center.

Visit the Moore House, one of the most historic rooms in America, where the terms for the surrender of Cornwallis were drawn up.

The Heart of Early History

down their arms. Tradition has it that they paraded to the tune of an old-time favorite, "The World Turned Upside Down." The title symbolized the arrival of a new nation with new ideas to change the tide of history.

Outside the battlefield, enroute back to Williamsburg via the parkway, the Yorktown Victory Center depicts, through exhibits and films, the story of the American Revolution from Concord to Yorktown. This is not part of the national park, but is operated by the Commonwealth of Virginia in conjunction with Jamestown Festival Park.

For Jamestown and Yorktown, the private restoration and re-creation of Colonial Williamsburg provides an important companion piece of history. When the statehouse at Jamestown burned for the fourth time in 1698, the capital was moved here to higher, healthier and safer ground. Williamsburg was a planned city, designed to reflect Virginia's pre-eminence among the colonies. And so it grew, as a center of culture and learning, as well as politics. For 80 years it was Virginia's capital (before the government was moved to Richmond). Now restored to its 18th century appearance, largely through the interest and initiative of the late John D. Rockefeller, Jr., Williamsburg comprises more than 400 public buildings, shops, homes and gardens, about half being original structures and the remainder, faithful reproductions on original sites. The historic area today, administered by the Colonial Williamsburg Foundation, is both a museum and living city, justifiably renowned throughout the world.

Cape Henry—the First Landing

At the mouth of Chesapeake Bay, 10 miles east of Norfolk and three miles north of Virginia Beach, the Jamestown colonists actually made their first landing at Cape Henry on April 26, 1607. Deeply impressed by the beauty of the setting, they lingered four days before proceeding upstream to found Jamestown. A quarter acre of land and a memorial cross mark the landing site, which lies within the boundaries of Fort Story Military Reservation. Cape Henry Memorial also memorializes the Battle of the Capes prior to the Battle of Yorktown, and has importance to both Jamestown *and* Yorktown.

Travel tips and tidbits

Picnic facilities are located along the Colonial Parkway at Great Neck, south of Williamsburg toward Jamestown; at Ringfield, midway between Williamsburg and Yorktown;

and along the York River beach in Yorktown. Park rangers patrolling the Parkway enforce the 45-mile per hour speed limit to ensure both public safety and enjoyment. Don't hesitate to ask them questions. There are no service stations along the route.

At Yorktown, a taped tour of the battlefield is available for a modest fee at the visitor center. Yorktown Day, commemorating the British surrender in 1781, is celebrated each year on October 19 with patriotic speeches, military displays, and with French representatives always in attendance.

At Williamsburg, you can rent a bicycle (at the Williamsburg Lodge) or bring your own for self-powered touring. Take the eight-mile country road winding through woodlands and traversing marshes and tidal creeks to Carter's Grove plantation, an outstanding attraction in its own right.

Campgrounds are located near Jamestown, on Route 31; in and around Williamsburg; and at Newport News Park, seven miles from Yorktown. There are no camping facilities in the national park.

While there are no accommodations at Jamestown, fast food is offered at adjacent Festival Park. Restaurants and overnight lodgings are available in Williamsburg and Yorktown. Among facilities operated by the Colonial Williamsburg Foundation, the Williamsburg Lodge (informal and fairly moderately priced) is just a few steps from the historic area. The Williamsburg Inn has hosted Queen Elizabeth, the Emperor of Japan, and U.S. Presidents. For the experience of a lifetime, stay at one of the colonial homes and taverns within the historic area operated in conjunction with the Inn. Peak periods are April (when gardens are their most glorious), summer, Thanksgiving and Christmas through New Year's Day; so plan early!

North to Fort McHenry

Fort McHenry National Monument and Historic Shrine, in Maryland, interprets a particular event, the writing of "The Star Spangled Banner," at a setting that makes it come alive as part of the flow of U.S. history. The Battle of Baltimore may not be considered epochal, yet it demonstrated to the world that this young upstart country was here to stay, for "the flag was still there."

Picture the time and place. Britain and France, warring against each other, both violated American neutrality by confiscating American ships and cargoes. Britain, in particular, impressed American seamen into its service. This, and political pressure to expand into British Canada and Spanish Florida, sparked the declaration of war in June, 1812. Two years later the British attacked and burned Washington, then moved on to the port of Baltimore.

The Heart of Early History

Fort McHenry, built in the late 1790s, guarded the approaches from the Patapsco River and Chesapeake Bay. In September 1814, the British unleashed a heavy 25-hour bombardment of the fort. As though dictated by fate, the action was witnessed from a vessel offshore by a young lawyer, Francis Scott Key, who had gone to secure the release of a friend from the British fleet. Until after midnight he observed the sky fiery with rockets and shells aimed at Fort McHenry. In the morning, when he saw the stars and stripes still waving over the fort, he began to write his immortal poem on the back of a letter.

Fort McHenry today is a showpiece of Baltimore harbor and easy to reach. Start your visit by viewing the 16-minute film in the visitor center auditorium. Then join park ranger-led activities (offered June 15 through Labor Day). A 30-minute tour explores the history of the star-shaped fort and

A "Star Spangled Banner" flies daily over Fort McHenry, as it did when Francis Scott Key saw it on the morning of September 14, 1814.

retraces the steps of those who manned it, through the officers' quarters, barracks, powder magazine, guardhouse and parade ground. From one of the bastions, the view of the Patapsco, where the British fleet lay at anchor while firing heavy explosives, clearly reveals Fort McHenry's strategic location.

Weekends in summer are made super-special by the Fort McHenry Guard, composed of volunteers who reenact history. The multi-part program begins at 1 p.m. each Saturday and Sunday with the ceremonial raising of a 15-star, 15-strip flag, a replica of the flag flying over the fort during the summer of 1814. Once the flag is raised, half the soldiers are dismissed to their barracks, while the remaining men are assigned to guard duty at various locations in the fort.

You can see them at their posts, tested periodically for alertness, or in their barracks pursuing 1814-style leisure activities. Occasionally the roll of the drums calls them to assembly on the parade ground for musket drill or a cannon drill. Then at 5:30 p.m. the men march in formation before the flag is lowered and secured for the night. Guard members, well versed in the history of the fort and the everyday lives of soldiers who manned it, are more than willing to answer questions of visitors. It's a treat to see them in their distinctive uniforms and to hear them explain how they prepared for the fierce attack, as though it has only lately happened.

Fort McHenry tells still another story. Used as a prison for Confederate soldiers during the Civil War and an Army hospital during World War I, it was designated a national monument in 1925—six years before "The Star Spangled Banner" was chosen as the national anthem. An island of green in the heart of industrial Baltimore, the park is surrounded by water on three sides and is frequented by a variety of birds during both spring and fall migration. This habitat offers good winter birding for northern water birds and gulls.

Travel tips and tidbits

Enjoy a stroll, jog or bike ride around Fort McHenry's seawall path. Or relax in the picnic area, near the statue of Orpheus, for lunch or dinner.

Baltimore's harbor has become one of the liveliest places along the East Coast. Narrated cruises aboard the **Defender** *or* **Guardian** *depart almost hourly for Fort McHenry from the Inner Harbor, with an opportunity to see many points of interest enroute. You can also drive directly to the fort on well-marked routes or reach it by bus; it's located at the end of MTA (Mass Transit Administration) Route #1.*

The Heart of Early History

The frigate **Constellation** *at Pier 1 in the Inner Harbor was built in 1797 and used against pirates in Tripoli in 1802 and against the British in 1812. Now it's considered the oldest ship in the world still afloat.*

During Historic Harbor House Tour in March, a number of choice homes in Fell's Point and Federal Hill near the harbor are open to the public.

While in the Baltimore area, plan to visit Hampton National Historic Site, preserving an elaborate Georgian mansion and landscaped grounds, in suburban Towson. Hampton is treated in detail in Tour III.

Valley Forge—"Crucible of Victory"

Twenty miles west of Philadelphia, Valley Forge National Historical Park conveys the sense of suffering and sacrifice endured by common soldiers during the Revolution. Washington's army of 12,000 men went into camp on December 19, 1777 and made it through a harsh and hungry winter to emerge in the spring as a trained, disciplined force the British henceforth would heed and respect.

George Washington himself had chosen this location, named for a small iron forge on Valley Creek, because of its defensive position and his ability

Thanks to a cooperative agreement with the Valley Forge Historical Society, the Sleeping Marquee used by George Washington is displayed in the visitor center.

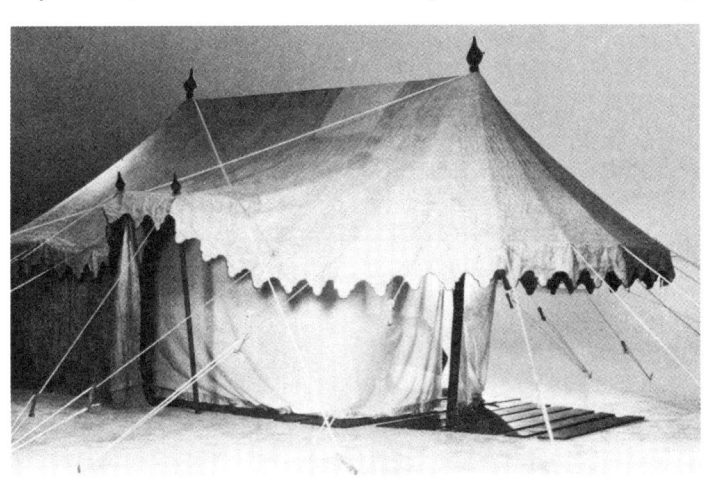

to watch the approaches from Philadelphia. The park is now a 3,000-acre scenic pleasure in any season of the year; during that winter, however, more than 1,500 men died as a consequence of disease and poor sanitation.

Exhibits in the visitor center recount the story of that harsh winter encampment. Take in the audiovisual program and displays; allow plenty of time to see such priceless items as an original tent used by Washington in the field and the celebrated Neumann Collection. These 18th century muskets, rifles, swords and other revolutionary weapons were acquired through the cooperation of the National Park Service, the Friends of Valley Forge and the generosity of The Sun Company.

While at the visitor center, you can choose your way of touring the park. You can purchase tickets for the bus tour, which operates on a regular schedule mid-April through October. It includes a taped narration and stops at principal sites. The fee is well worth it, and you can leave your car at the visitor center. Or you can drive the route in your own car, using park maps or rented tapes to guide you. The maps are available in the bookstore along with a wide range of publications on Valley Forge and the Revolution. The bookstore is operated by the Valley Forge Park Interpretive Association, a not-for profit organization which supports park activities. You'll find interpreters on duty at major locations.

Along the way, note the sites where many huts were built (estimates range from 800 to 2,000) of logs and sod. Forty-three have been reconstructed throughout the park, including a cluster where Brigadier General Peter Muhlenberg's brigade manned the eastern end of the outer line of defense. Throughout the summer, and on weekends the rest of the year, interpreters in costume demonstrate soldier life at the Muhlenberg Huts. The Memorial Arch, a dominant feature of the park, commemorates the "incomparable patience and fidelity of the soldiery"—the men who departed here in the spring of 1778 for the Battle of Monmouth as a toughened fighting force.

Reconstructed huts and costumed interpreters mark the site where General Muhlenberg's Brigade manned the outer line of defense.

The Heart of Early History

The National Memorial Arch commemorates the "patience and fidelity" of the soldiers who wintered at Valley Forge in 1777-78.

The arch is one of several powerful memorials in stone and bronze. Others include the mounted figure of General Anthony Wayne, in the area where he commanded the Pennsylvania troops, and the somber, towering Friedrich von Steuben, the Prussian who could barely speak English yet trained the troops to be efficient and proud. It is not too difficult to picture the scene of May 6, 1778 on the level greensward called the Grand Parade, when the Army paraded to celebrate the newly announced alliance with France. Cannons boomed, thousands of muskets were fired, and cheers echoed across the fields. This army, having survived the "Winter Encampment," was ready for the future.

The principal personality giving inspiration at Valley Forge, as throughout the war, was George Washington. From the day he took command of the armies in 1775, his faith in the rightness of the cause never wavered. Though he pleaded for support, Congress frequently failed to provide it. Nevertheless, at the Potts House, his headquarters which still stands, he shared the seasons with his men.

Adjacent to the park on private land, the Washington Memorial Chapel is well worth seeing for its beautiful stained glass windows and wood carvings. Rest here a few moments in quiet contemplation, then visit the Chapel Auxiliary shop in a cabin at the rear; it offers a range of tasteful mementoes.

The focal point of Valley Forge camp activities, the Issac Potts House, was General and Mrs. Washington's quarters.

Travel tips and tidbits

Bring your bicycle or (during summer months) rent one and enjoy the six-mile paved trail. Stop for a picnic at one of the three areas in the park—Varnum's, Wayne's Woods, or Betzwood—or at the Washington Headquarters area where snacks and souvenirs are available.

Revolutionary War sites are scattered throughout this section of Pennsylvania and nearby New Jersey. One of them, at Morristown, NJ, is administered by the National Park Service, while the others are maintained by the states, counties, historical societies and other citizen groups. A short distance from Valley Forge, Waynesborough, the home of Brigadier General Anthony Wayne, is maintained by local citizens and is well interpreted. Valley Forge derives its name from a colonial ironworks. Pennsylvania, in fact, was by far the important iron manufacturing colony. Hopewell Furnace National Historic Site, the most completely restored ironmaking community, is located within an hour's drive of Valley Forge (about five miles south of Birdsboro on Pennsylvania Route 345).

Numerous hotels and motels are located in the Valley Forge area. The McIntosh Inn at King of Prussia is moderately priced; the Embassy Suites in Chesterbrook is one of the nicest. For information about overnight lodgings, camping, restaurants and motor routes, check at the visitor center. Ask about state parks (Pennsylvania has more than 100) and county parks.

Morristown—Where Lafayette brought welcome news

Barely 30 miles from New York, Morristown National Historical Park constitutes the companion piece to Valley Forge. It was the location of Washington's military headquarters and the main encampment of the

27

The Heart of Early History

Continental Army during the winters of 1777 and 1779-80—that is, before and after Valley Forge.

The winter of 1779 was particularly severe, the worst winter of the war. It saw thousands of men suffering from lack of shoes or stockings or food, ravaged by dysentery and assorted fevers (inoculations had reduced the danger of smallpox following the encampment here in 1777).

The place to begin is the museum at Washington's Headquarters in the heart of Morristown, displaying one of the country's most extensive and absorbing collections of military artifacts and Washingtoniana. Then visit the adjacent Ford Mansion, which served as Washington's headquarters. From here he reorganized his weary and depleted forces and welcomed Lafayette who brought word that a French army was on its way to aid the Americans. Some of the furniture now on display actually was in the Ford Mansion during Washington's occupancy; few kitchens anywhere, in fact, are so completely furnished with colonial utensils and equipment.

During the second Morristown encampment, Washington, his wife, aides-de-camp, and servants lived in the house of Jacob Ford.

A road leads from Morristown into the Fort Nonsense area of the park, a key orientation point. Jockey Hollow, five miles south of town, with rolling woodlands and open fields, closely resembles the setting when the main Continental Army of 10,000 prepared to encamp here for the winter of 1779-80. A visitor center provides orientation and exhibits about the life and times of the Continental Soldier. The wintering grounds have remained relatively undisturbed and reconstructed log cabins recall the times of the "hard winter."

Take special note of the Wick House, standing on the road to Mendham. It was a farm home that served as headquarters of General Arthur St. Clair, commander of the Pennsylvania Line. The kitchen garden, a project of the Herb Society of America, is a feature in itself, with its herbs, quince tree,

The Wick House, in the Jockey Hollow area, was surrounded by some 1,100 log huts used by the officers and men during the severe winter at Morristown.

and rows of gooseberry and currants before the background of fruit trees, the whole ensemble recreating the 18th century scene.

Nature, both cultivated and wild, is much a part of this park. More than 100 species of birds, some 20 species of mammals, and 300 species of shrubs, trees and wildflowers have been identified in Jockey Hollow and the New Jersey Brigade Unit of the park. A walk over any of the 27 miles of hiking trails affords the opportunity to experience the indivisible natural and historical park landscape.

Travel tips and tidbits

New Jersey has been called the "cockpit of the Revolution," with so many battles and skirmishes (more than 100) that a visitor might think the whole war was fought in this little land. On Christmas night of 1777, Washington and his beleaguered army crossed the ice-clogged Delaware from what is now called Washington Crossing State Park of Pennsylvania. It lies about 7½ miles southeast of New Hope and is well worth a visit. But that's only the beginning.

Washington debarked at what is now Washington Crossing State Park of New Jersey, paused at the little ferry house before advancing with his 2,400 troops through snow and sleet to attack the Hessians at Trenton. The two state parks are now connected by a bridge. The Ferry House on the Jersey side has been restored as a colonial inn. The Flag Museum, at the entrance to Continental Lane, depicts the evolution of the American flag from the time of the early explorers to the present.

After crossing the ice-clogged Delaware, Washington surprised and attacked the Hessian garrison at Trenton, capturing about 1,000 prisoners. But reinforcements dispatched by Cornwallis arrived to engage the colonial forces in the Second Battle of Trenton. The Old Barracks, on South Willow and Front Streets, dating from 1758, are considered among the finest specimens of colonial barracks in the country; they were occupied variously by British, Hessian and Continental troops and by Tory refugees.

The Heart of Early History

Following the action at Trenton, Washington withdrew to Princeton. The university there was already established and operating; but Nassau Hall was used as barracks and hospital by both British and colonial troops. In 1783 the Continental Congress met in Nassau Hall when mutinous American soldiers drove its members from Philadelphia. But there was a happy side to it; while at Nassau Hall, Congress received the news of the treaty of peace with Britain.

Fort Necessity—Coming from the West

Near Uniontown, Pennsylvania, about an hour's drive, south of Pittsburgh on Route 40, Fort Necessity National Battlefield preserves the site of George Washington's first major military encounter, well before the Revolutionary War. It was on a rainy July 3, 1754 when an untested young colonel (then only 22) led his force of Virginia volunteers, accompanied by South Carolina regulars, against a superior force of French soldiers and their Indian allies. This seemingly obscure event in the remote North American wilderness was destined to have worldwide repercussions.

The reconstructed stockaded fort, which Washington built out of necessity (hence the name "Fort Necessity"), stands as a reminder of the battle fought for control of the Ohio River Valley. Young Washington called the Great Meadows "a charming field for an encounter." Nevertheless, after nine hours of fighting, he was forced to surrender to the French. This action, deeply resented by England, sparked a series of events leading to the conflict known in North America as the French and Indian War. Subse-

Costumed interpreters relate the events of July 1754 beside the circular stockade of logs - Washington's Fort Necessity.

quently this engagement led to the struggle in Europe and elsewhere known as the Seven Years' War. It would end in 1763, with the expulsion of French power from North America and India.

At the visitor center, exhibits and the orientation film will help you to understand the battle fought here and its pivotal role in history. You'll learn how park historians carefully researched details of the original fort built by Washington in 1754 and how these findings, coupled with archaeological discoveries, made the present replica possible. Several miles of hiking trails and a small picnic area (including facilities for the handicapped) are available.

Mount Washington Tavern, within walking distance of Fort Necessity, was built in 1828 when the country was expanding westward, into the territory claimed by France until the French and Indian War. Standing in front of the tavern, you can face modern U.S. Route 40. It's a reminder of the early days of the republic when the National Road passed here. The tavern, in fact, typifies the combination hotel-restaurant built during the 1820s, the days of stagecoach travel. Exhibits and guided tours of the well preserved tavern will help you understand the course of growth along the first federally built route west. The National Road was the inspiration of Albert Gallatin, Swiss immigrant and statesman.

Mount Washington Tavern, built as a stage stop on the Old National Pike overlooks the site of Fort Necessity.

Be sure to see two detached, but nearby, parts of the park:

Jumonville Glen, about 7½ miles distant, was the scene of a preliminary skirmish between Washington and a French patrol. Now it provides the setting of a delightful scenic walk.

Braddock's grave, about one mile west of the fort, marks the burial place of General Edward Braddock, who commanded the British Army in America in 1755. Braddock was mortally wounded at the Battle of the Monongahela

31

and brought here for burial during the British retreat. Alongside the memorial monument a fragment of the Braddock Road, the route through the wilderness, has been preserved.

Travel tips and tidbits

The Uniontown area is a good place to slow down and tarry awhile. About 25 miles to the southwest of Fort Necessity, Friendship Hill National Historic Site nestles on a scenic plateau of the Laurel Mountains. Friendship Hill, the country estate of Albert Gallatin, is treated in detail in Chapter VI.

Fallingwater, one of Frank Lloyd Wright's most famous houses, lies about 13 miles northeast of Fort Necessity on Pennsylvania Route 381. It was designed in 1936 and built over a waterfall. A panel of distinguished architects recently voted it to be the most significant American building in the last 100 years. Guided tours (offered April through November daily except Monday) will give you the opportunity to judge for yourself.

Ohiopyle State Park, just six miles northeast of Fort Necessity on Route 381, includes facilities for fishing, whitewater boating, hiking, camping, bicycling, cross-country skiing and snowmobiling in a mountain forest.

On to Philadelphia—Independence Declared

Principles of self-government and self-determination by nations are memorialized in the Philadelphia downtown area called "the most historic square mile in America." Preserved here are the very settings where the Continental Congress met and governed the colonies during the bitter, trying days of the Revolution; where the Declaration of Independence and Constitution were conceived and adopted; and where Congress and the Supreme Court conducted their affairs for ten years before the capital of the nation was moved to the new city to be named Washington.

Philadelphia, once a tiny hamlet in the wilderness, became William Penn's "Greene Countrie Towne," the gateway to Pennsylvania, or Penn's Woods. Then it grew into *the* metropolis of English America, a fitting birthplace for the Republic in 1776. Independence Square comprises the most extensive and complex restoration ever undertaken by government—a combined federal, state and city effort—emphasized anew during the 200th anniversary of the U.S. Constitution.

There is, in fact, much more to Independence National Historical Park than its two best known landmarks—the Liberty Bell and Independence Hall. Plan to view movies and portraits, to explore restored houses, churches and

Independence Hall where in 1776 delegates from 13 colonies declared their independence, and where 11 years later delegates adopted the Constitution of the United States.

military museums, and to stop for lunch or dinner, if you wish, at a reconstructed historic tavern.

In block after block, the visitor can see historic and architectural monuments that figured in the flowering of independence. The development of the 20-acre park has involved the demolition of 100 worn and faded structures, including one 10-story building, and replacing them with greensward, trees, walks, walls, and gates, such as those that stood here long ago. This restoration tells the story of Philadelphia as well as the nation; for the city stepped in to rescue Independence Hall and Square in 1818, when it was

The Heart of Early History

proposed to parcel out land for building plots, and it continues to hold title to them.

The place to begin is the modern, brick visitor center at Third and Chestnut Streets. It is actually an orientation center, with important things to do *before* touring the park. See the film *Independence*, directed by John Huston, in the visitor center auditorium; it brings history to life. Pick up pamphlets and maps, and tickets to the Bishop White and Dolly Todd Houses. Learn about daily special events, where and when they take place. Ask questions of park rangers and volunteer park aids, who are always glad to help.

Plan your time, but allow some time for surprises and discoveries. At the visitor center, for instance, you can see the pet eagle of Charles Willson Peale, the famous early portrait artist. When the country was born, the bird was alive and well. Later it was stuffed, and perched for years atop the Liberty Bell in Independence Hall.

The main building to visit, of course, is Independence Hall. Once, as capitol of Pennsylvania, it was the most impressive building in the colonies. It remains impressive today, restored to its original Georgian beauty. But that's a story in itself, for Independence Hall has been pieced together anew after precarious years when ceilings sagged and walls neared collapse. As part of the restoration, skilled technicians performed patient, minute work, taking apart brick walls and wood paneling, studying them piece by piece; historians examined many manuscripts in this country and in the British Museum.

Among the original furnishings in the Assembly Room (Independence Hall) are the "rising sun" chair and the Syng ink stand.

The Assembly Room, refurnished with original and authentic period items, appears substantially the same as in 1776, when delegates adopted the Declaration of Independence. The two most famous pieces are the "rising sun" chair, which Washington occupied during the Constitutional Convention, and the silver inkstand on the President's desk, used by the delegates to sign both the Declaration of Independence and Constitution. The way to see Independence Hall—the *only* way, in fact—is on a guided tour. Tours begin from the East Wing usually about every 15 minutes, but it may be every 10, 20 or 30 minutes, depending on the number of visitors.

Congress Hall, next door, has also been restored, looking the way John Adams found it for his inauguration. Two other significant buildings in this harmoniously styled cluster are Philosophical Hall, headquarters of the American Philosophical Society, the country's oldest learned society, and Old City Hall, where the U.S. Supreme Court met while Philadelphia was the nation's capital. Library Hall, across the street from Independence Square, houses major historical collections (such as Benjamin Franklin's

The Liberty Bell, traditionally associated with events of the American Revolution, has become an international symbol of freedom.

The Heart of Early History

papers and the journals of Lewis and Clark) for scholarly research. Library Hall as it now exists is a reconstruction (with a wing added).

Cross Chestnut Street to the striking glass and stone pavilion housing the Liberty Bell. The bell was originally orderd from England in 1751 as a memorial to William Penn's "Charter of Privileges." However, the bell played its most dramatic role on July 8, 1776, when it tolled to summon citizens to the first public reading of the Declaration of Independence. During the Civil War members of the Abolitionist Movement, a group which denounced slavery, took the bell and its inscription as their symbol and coined the phrase, "Liberty Bell." From that time on it has been a worldwide symbol of liberty.

The bell was integral to Independence Hall until the early hours of 1976 when the National Park Service, as part of the nation's Bicentennial, moved it to its new home to permit easier viewing. This is one feature of the park to be seen at any time of day or night. For the after-dark visitor, the pavilion is illuminated, though not open. From the outside, you can push a button and hear a taped account of the bell's history through the years.

History and architecture are both attractions of the park, the architecture enhancing the feeling of times past. The Second Bank of the United States, for example, is a Greek Revival classic that once housed an important financial institution. Since 1974 it has displayed a gallery of portraits dedicated to the founders of the country, thus it is a respository of both art and history. For the year 1987, however, the Second Bank is devoted to a major display, "Miracle at Philadelphia," marking the 200th anniversary of the Constitution.

The Second Bank of the United States, normally an American portrait gallery, features a five year exhibit on the Constitution.

By walking to Franklin Court, on the south side of Market Street, you can see the results of archaeological digging at the site of the home Benjamin Franklin built in 1765 and where he died in 1790. The building is long gone, but a ramp leads to an underground museum featuring sophisticated displays and devices that would have intrigued Old Ben himself. You'll learn more about Franklin and sites associated with him in the Great Americans Tour, Chapter VI.

The Bishop White House, on Walnut Street, once occupied by "the father of the American Protestant Episcopal Church," represents an excellent example of an early Philadelphia row house. Today's visitor may find it difficult to believe that until recent years the front parlor and dining room were used as offices; yet the National Park Service has succeeded in its complete restoration, with many original furnishings contributed by descendants of Bishop White.

A few doors away, the Dolley Todd House, where Dolley Madison lived with her first husband, has also been restored and authentically refurnished, including the first-floor law office where John Todd practiced, and the upstairs parlor, where the widowed Dolley Todd would later receive James Madison, known as "the great little Madison." Tickets for the Bishop White and Todd Houses should be obtained before leaving the visitor center; they're both relatively small houses and the number of daily visitors is limited.

Other focal points of the Revolutionary era include the three-story reconstructed Graff House, where Thomas Jefferson stayed while writing the Declaration of Independence, and the house once occupied by General Thaddeus Kosciuszko. You can plan to have a meal at the reconstructed City Tavern, a restaurant serving 18th century fare. Because of its popularity, reservations are suggested, especially in the summer.

Several churches and cemeteries are part of the historical complex, too. St. Joseph's was established in 1733 as the first Catholic church in Philadelphia (the present church is the third on the site). St. Mary's principal Catholic church during the Revolution, has an interesting graveyard, including the tomb of Admiral John Barry, "father of the American Navy." So has Christ Church, where Benjamin Franklin and six other signers of the Declaration of Independence are buried. At Mikveh Israel Cemetery, the oldest Jewish burial ground in the city, Haym Salomon, patriot and financier of the Revolution, is interred. Nine blocks south of Independence Hall, Gloria Dei is a reminder that the Swedes preceded the English to this part of the New World and began their congregation as early as 1646. The present structure, built in 1700, is the oldest church in Philadelphia.

The Heart of Early History

The reconstructed City Tavern, 2nd Street at Walnut Street, serves today's visitors in the manner of yesteryears' delegates, with 18th century candlelight and charm.

The Deshler-Morris House, another unit of the park, is located in the Germantown section of Philadelphia, seven miles from Independence Hall. It served as Washington's home in November of 1793 and the summer of 1794. The restored house is now considered an outstanding example of Georgian architecture. Nearby Cliveden, another Georgian showpiece, was occupied by British troops in October 1777; it is administered by the National Trust for Historic Preservation.

Travel tips and tidbits

Most park buildings are open 9 a.m. to 5 p.m. daily, but during the summer, hours are extended at some of them. From early May to Labor Day, waiting time for tours of Independence Hall may range from 15 minutes to one hour. Thursday and Friday are peak days in April, May and June, because of school groups. Come on other weekdays if you can.

If you're driving, park in the garage on 2nd Street, between Chestnut and Walnut, one block from the visitor center. Otherwise, the park can easily be reached by bus, subway or taxi.

It's better to see a few points of interest in leisure than to try to see everything in haste. Make a list of places in the park that most appeal to you and budget your time accordingly. Park rangers at the visitor center will help. You can (and should!) come back another time.

Pick up a list of daily activities. These change from year to year, but sometimes include outdoor plays, or walking tours devoted to Franklin's life and influence or to James Madison's haunts. Special events during the year include Philadelphia Open House, a series of neighborhood tours sponsored by Friends of Independence National Historical Park the first three weeks in May, and the Fourth of July, when various activities are listed in the daily papers. On July 8, you can join in the commemoration of the reading of the Declaration of Independence behind Independence Hall.

Picnicking is allowed throughout the park, and street vendors provide a wide range of fare. For your picnic stop, consider Welcome Park, an outdoor museum commemorating the founding of Pennsylvania in 1682 by William Penn. Penn's life as a Quaker and plans for his "Greene Countrie Towne" are described on panels marking the plaza.

For more substantial food service, the City Tavern, across Second Street from Welcome Park, has been rebuilt by the National Park Service to appear as it did 200 years ago— even down to the front awning which shielded the tavern from summer sun. The National Park Service and Nilon, Inc., the tavern's operator, both hope that should John Adams return he would still regard the City Tavern as "the most genteel one in America."

Evening makes a choice time for a walking tour, especially in summer. "Twilight Tours," conducted by Friends of Independence National Historical Park, afford a choice opportunity. Visitors and local residents alike find pleasure in browsing along little streets like Delancey, Pine and Lombard in the Society Hill section, where the environment of another era pervades. Not all the houses are old, or even simulated antique, but the most modern are in scale, enhancing the human dimension.

The Heart of Early History

Park Information

Fort McHenry National Monument and Historic Shrine
Baltimore, MD 21230-5393
(301) 962-4290

Visitor Center—Take I-95 to Baltimore, exit at Key Highway/Fort McHenry exit. Follow signs to the Monument. The Visitor Center is located next to the main parking lot.

Visitor Center hours 8:00—4:45 Daily; 8:00—7:45 Mid June to Labor Day

Fort Necessity National Battlefield
The National Pike
RD 2, Box 528
Farmington, PA 15437
(412) 329-5512

Visitor Center—11 miles east of Uniontown, PA along U.S. Route 40.

Visitor Center hours Daily 10:30 am—5:00 pm (Closed Thanksgiving, Christmas, New Years)

Independence National Historical Park
313 Walnut Street
Philadelphia, PA 19106
(215) 597-8974 or 75

Visitor Center—3rd & Chestnut Streets. Each of the following sets of directions will lead you to the parking garage on 2nd Street between Chestnut and Walnut Streets. **Eastbound** via I-76 (Schuylkill Expressway): Exit at Vine Street (I-676 and U.S. 30) and follow to 6th Street. Turn right on 6th and follow to Chestnut (3 blocks). Turn left on Chestnut and follow to 2nd Street. Turn right on 2nd Street. **Westbound** via Benjamin Franklin Bridge (U.S. 30): As you come off the bridge, follow the signs to 6th Street (south). From there, follow the same directions as outlined for Eastbound to reach 2nd Street. **Southbound** via I-95: Take the Center City exit to 2nd Street. **Northbound** via I-95: Exit at Tasker Street. Continue straight ahead to Reed Street. Turn right on Reed and follow to Delaware Avenue. Turn left on Delaware Avenue and follow to the exit for Market Street (on right). When you reach Market, make an immediate left onto 2nd Street.

Visitor Center hours 9—5 (Sept.—June); 9—6 (July & August)

Jamestown National Historical Site
c/o Colonial National Historical Park
P.O. Box 210
Yorktown, Virginia 23690
(804) 229-1733

Visitor Center—Located on Jamestown Island, nine miles southwest of Williamsburg, Virginia, via the scenic Colonial Parkway.

Visitor Center hours 9:00—5:00 winter, 9:00—5:30 summer

Morristown National Historical Park
Washington Place
Morristown, NJ 07960
(201) 539-2016

Visitor Center—Route 287 to Exit 32 (Washington's Headquarters), left onto Morris St., follow to Washington's Headquarters parking.

Visitor Center hours 9:00—5:00, Wed—Sun

Valley Forge National Historical Park
Valley Forge, Pennsylvania 19481
(215) 783-7700

Visitor Center—Located at the intersection of PA Route #23 and North Gulph Road (between King of Prussia, PA and Valley Forge, PA)

Visitor Center hours 8:30—5:00 (except Christmas Day)

Yorktown Battlefield
c/o Colonial National Historical Park
P.O. Box 210
Yorktown, Virginia 23690
(804) 898-3400

Visitor Center—Located at Yorktown, Virginia, thirteen miles east of Williamsburg, Virginia, via Colonial Parkway.

Visitor Center hours 8:30—5:00 winter; 8:30—5:30 summer

In the Moore House near Yorktown, a costumed park ranger relates the story of the terms and surrender of British General Cornwallis in 1781.

Tour Two
1. Shenandoah National Park and Skyline Drive
2. Blue Ridge Parkway
3. New River Gorge National River
4. Delaware Water Gap National Recreation Area
5. Upper Delaware Scenic and Recreational River
6. Hampton National Historic Site
7. Assateague Island National Seashore
8. Pinelands National Reserve

Additional Sights
(A) Hawks Nest State Park
(B) Pipestem State Park
(C) Stokes, Worthington State Forests
(D) Assateague State Park
(E) Chincoteague National Wildlife Refuge
(F) Brigantine National Wildlife Refuge
(G) Barnegat National Wildlife Refuge

Tour Two

From the Mountains to the Sea
A Tour of Rivers and Wild Nature

Natural areas in the Mid-Atlantic states range from barrier coastal islands, sand beaches and marshes to portions of the ancient mountains of Appalachia, luxuriant with wildflowers, waterfalls and free-flowing streams. Visitors are surprised and pleased to discover the variety and quality of wild nature, so readily accessible from large population centers.

Much wilderness has been lost in the spread of industries and cities, yet national parks have been established to save these areas as "islands of hope" for human inspiration and recreation. The wisdom in doing so is clearly evident by their popularity.

Shenandoah National Park, VA is the oldest national park visited on this tour. It was first approved by Congress in 1926, at a time when Acadia, in Maine, was the only national park east of the Mississippi. But complete acceptance depended upon the people of Virginia acquiring the land and deeding it to the federal government; for, unlike the western parks, these

From the Mountains to the Sea

weren't public lands, but privately owned mostly by struggling mountain farmers. It took almost 10 years to realize the dream, but the enthusiasm and energy of Virginians would not be denied and the park was dedicated on July 3, 1936 by President Franklin D. Roosevelt.

The other areas are much newer additions to the National Park System. They, too, reflected the awareness and interest of local citizens, supported by many others elsewhere, even at great distances, who recognized nature's special values and wanted to preserve them.

Almost all of these parks could be considered destinations in themselves, rather than points of interest on a tour. They do, however, group together logically by location and landscape. For instance, the southern Appalachian mountains and rivers are the common themes of Shenandoah National Park, the Blue Ridge Parkway and New River Gorge National River.

Though deep in the mountains of Virginia, Shenandoah lies less than 100 miles from Washington or Baltimore, less than a day's drive from New York or Cleveland. For a distance of 105 miles, the Skyline Drive stretches like a ribbon, crossing and recrossing the ridgetop of Shenandoah. At Rockfish Gap, between Charlottesville and Waynesboro, the road changes in name to the Blue Ridge Parkway and continues for the next 469 miles to the Great Smoky Mountains—constituting the longest road in the world designed strictly for scenic enjoyment. In West Virginia, (2 hours from Lexington, VA, and on I-64) the New River Gorge National River embraces a spectacular 52-mile stretch of an ancient river that still runs free and untamed, with rapids to challenge the most daring of kayakers.

Another river and other mountains are common to two national park units easily reached from Philadelphia and New York. Delaware Water Gap National Recreation Area, between the Kittatinny Ridge in New Jersey and Pocono Mountain Plateau in Pennsylvania, includes about 35 miles of the long, narrow Delaware River Valley. The 73-mile stretch of the Upper Delaware Scenic and Recreational River flows through forested and rolling country between the Poconos and the Catskills of New York. Between them they furnish sport and pleasure for fishermen, canoeists, kayakers, birders, artists, and followers of old canals and older Indian paths.

On the Atlantic seaboard, southeast of Washington and Baltimore, Assateague Island National Seashore—a complex of sand beaches and dunes, marshes and flocks of wild birds—comprises the largest undeveloped seashore between Massachusetts and North Carolina. Pinelands National Reserve is close to the coast, in a setting of cedar swamps and pine-oak forest. Hampton National Historic Site, MD, while not preserving nature in the wild like the other parks, does represent in its suburban

Baltimore gardens and grounds humankind's harmony with nature. As Henry Winthrop Sargent wrote in 1859, "It has truly been said of Hampton that it expresses more grandeur than any other place in America."

Note the mile markers placed on the side of Skyline Drive, numbered from north to south, to help you find features, facilities, and services.

Shenandoah—Astride the Forested Blue Ridge

Shenandoah National Park is set in a natural refuge in hills of hardwood and pine forests, and open meadows, with vistas of gentle valleys and mountains beyond them to the western horizon. The Skyline Drive, a mountaintop road, is a motoring delight, meant for stopping and exploring in leisure, rather than non-stop driving in haste.

You could easily cover the full length of the drive, 105 miles, within a day, but you'd miss the significance of it. Plan to stay at least one or two nights at a lodge, motel or campground (either inside or outside the park). The drive provides access to 500 miles of trail, ranging from short leisurely walks to long-distance hikes over the Appalachian Trail (extending 2,100 miles from Maine to Georgia). Birders find more than 200 species at one time or another during the year, while wildflower enthusiasts may identify as many as 80 flowering plants in a day's walk.

It pays to drive at a slower pace, within the speed limit or below it, for both touring enjoyment and safety. You never know when a deer may jump into the road. Or, you might round a curve and find a car stopped in the middle of your lane while the driver takes a photograph or while the passengers stare at a circling hawk.

Four main entrances lead to the park and Skyline Drive. From the north entrance, near Front Royal, stop at Dickey Ridge Visitor Center (Mile 4.6)

President and Mrs. Hoover's fishing camp, built before the establishment of the park, was later donated to the federal government.

for exhibits describing park attractions, facilities and activities. Here you can learn about picnic areas and scenic overlooks, guided hikes, evening campfire programs, campgrounds and accommodations, and special sights of the season.

Plan to visit the Harry F. Byrd, Sr. Visitor Center at Big Meadows (Mile 51), named for a prominent Virginia governor and U.S. senator who knew the park intimately and championed it. Byrd was governor during the park's formative years. He and George Freeman Pollack, colorful owner of the mountaintop Skyland resort, played key roles in raising funds to purchase land for the park.

From the developed area at Skyland, hike the 1½-mile, round-trip Stony Man Nature Trail, a leisurely path leading through a good cross-section of the nearly 100 species of trees in the park. It ascends to a craggy 4,010-foot summit, perched 3,000 feet above Shenandoah Valley. That's a "shortie." The circuit hike to Camp Hoover is longer, a little over six miles from Big Meadows wayside, but it's easy and scenic all the way. It leads to the old lodge on the Rapidan River that Herbert Hoover built when he was president, before the park was established. The camp is surprisingly simple, but it served Hoover's purpose: to break away from Washington and fish the quiet pools and riffles.

The 7.7 mile circuit hike to Old Rag Mountain—"Old Raggedy"—is tough and takes a full day (from near the little town of Nethers, outside the park), but it leads to Shenandoah's most spectacular and fascinating peak. Hikers love it because of the unique Ridge Trail, winding around massive boulders and through a cave before reaching the summit with expansive views in all directions.

Bearface Mountain - the park is a hicker's paradise with over 200 miles of foot trails; take time to stop, look, listen and explore.

    The Appalachian Trail follows the mountain crest for 94 miles through the park, with numerous spur trails. You can take a stretch of the "AT" in small or large measures, for an hour, a half-day, or the full length and then some on the way from Georgia to Mt. Katahdin, the northern terminus in Maine.

    If you're not used to hiking, beware of starting an all-day trip from the trail's upper end on the Drive. The first half will probably be downhill and easy; but the return trip, when the day may be hot and the hiker tired, will be uphill and steep.

    Shenandoah is a park for all seasons. Spring flowers and budding trees begin their show in late March. By mid-April magenta-colored redbud floods the valleys, followed by creamy white dogwood, pink azalea and pink and white mountain laurel, with flowers in profusion well into June. During summer, the temperature usually is 15 degrees cooler than in the valley below. By mid-September, foliage begins its autumn color change, reaching a peak in October and gradually flowing downward from mountain tops to coves and hollows.

    In late spring and summer, the woods are filled with the tunes of wrens, warblers, thrushes, tanagers and other songbirds. The sharp-eyed, light treading visitor is apt to spot a wild turkey, especially in the northern part of the park. Common ravens, rare in eastern United States, are residents of

From the Mountains to the Sea

A winter weekend or holiday at Shenandoah National Park offers many rewarding experiences.

Shenandoah. Soaring birds—hawks, vultures and ravens—are often seen riding air currents over mountaintops and valleys.

Winter offers a special treat, especially after a snow or ice storm. On cold, crispy days evergreens stand out boldly against snowy white mountains, while icicles cascade over the cliffs. It takes a little effort, and proper clothing, to prepare for winter, but it's well worth it. The central section of the park road is kept open through the winter months, if at all possible—especially the section from U.S. 211 (Thornton Gap) to Big Meadows. If the drive should be closed by snow or ice, try hiking or skiing along the drive or trails.

Under normal conditions, visitors can touch and feel the high country by stepping into it from 75 parking overlooks along the Skyline Drive. At Hogback 11 bends of the Shenandoah are visible, and no two overlooks are ever the same. They enable one to photograph dawn over the Piedmont Plain stretching eastward, to hike the wilderness where streams tumble into waterfalls—roaring in spring, frozen in winter—and to count the golden shadows spreading over the Shenandoah Valley.

Travel tips and tidbits

Campgrounds are located at Mathews Arm (northern section), Big Meadows and Lewis Mountain (central section), and Loft Mountain (southern section), with a 14-day limit in effect June 1 to October 31. During the summer season plenty of space is available midweek, but weekends and holidays are crowded. You can reserve a site at Big Meadows, the largest and most popular campground, at any Ticketron outlet; the other three operate first-come first served.

Overnight lodging and restaurants are at Skyland and Big Meadows, plus housekeeping cabins at Lewis Mountain. Reservations are desirable early April through October. Write ARA Virginia Sky-Line Company, Box 727, Luray, VA 22835, or call 703-743-5108. Food service and gasoline are available at Elkwallow Wayside, Panorama, Big Meadows and Loft Mountain.

Since the national park is long but very narrow, facilities outside its borders are easily reached. Front Royal, at the northern entrance, and Waynesboro, at the southern entrance, offer many motels, restaurants and campgrounds. Luray, on U.S. 211 just west of the park, has plenty of tourist facilities. On the east side of the park, Graves Mountain Lodge (Syria, VA 82743) is a well established and popular family-owned resort for people who enjoy mountain beauty and good food. At Charlottesville the charming, but rather expensive Boar's Head Inn is located within easy reach of the beautiful "Monticello," Thomas Jefferson's hilltop home and gardens (open for public tours). On the west side of the park, Shenandoah Countryside (Route 2, Box 377, Luray, VA 22835), operated by Phil and Bob Jacobsen, offers outstanding "bread and breakfast" accommodations, plus magnificent vistas, and a traditional wood-fired sauna. Winchester, Harrisonburg, Charlottesville, Staunton and historic Lexington, site of Washington and Lee University, are within driving range and have plenty of tourist facilities.

A white-tailed deer stands momentarily; deer, foxes, bears, bobcats, and other smaller mammals roam the forests of Shenandoah.

From the Mountains to the Sea

Try to make it for Hoover Days, held the August weekend closest to Herbert Hoover's birthday, August 10. The schedule includes special programs and exhibits at the Byrd Visitor Center at Big Meadows and guided tours of all the buildings at Camp Hoover. Buses run at frequent intervals from Big Meadows; you can ride both ways or hike one way and ride the other. (Incidentally, Herbert Hoover's birthplace, at West Branch, IA, is a very attractive national historic site—keep it in mind for some future trip.)

October weekends can be crowded, especially at the height of the foliage season. You can expect bumper-to-bumper traffic. As an alternative, consider exploring paved secondary roads on east or west sides of the park. Or drive through the northern part of the Massanutten Range, reached by driving west of Front Royal or Luray; it's a lovely area considered years ago as a potential national park.

For local information on special events, contact the Luray Chamber of Commerce (703-743-3915).

Consider a side trip to Harper's Ferry National Historical Park, WV, the site of John Brown's ill-fated abolitionist raid. (See the Chapter map.)

Attempted feeding of black bears, or other wild animals, can result in human injury. Feeding represents misguided kindness.

Down the Blue Ridge the Scenic Way

At Rockfish Gap, the Skyline Drive dips from the mountain crest and then climbs again, continuing south as the Blue Ridge Parkway into North Carolina and the Great Smoky Mountains. In some sections the parkway runs along the very crest of the mountains. Vistas from the overlooks are never the same; allow plenty of time for them. Sample, at least, the excellent hiking trails, from short leg-stretchers to steep climbs, and include a little of the Appalachian Trail which roughly parallels the parkway north of Roanoke.

After driving to Rockfish Gap on the Skyline Drive, you don't have to go far to reach Humpback Rocks, at the northern end of the parkway, where the self-guiding trail weaves among a cluster of log buildings of pioneer days. Should you continue south, you'll come to the James River Overlook, high above one of America's historic rivers, where exhibits and a restored lock tell the story of the old Kanawha Canal.

Late September and early October are prime spans for observing southerly migration of many birds and butterflies from overlooks along the parkway. From Milepost 92, near the Peaks of Otter, hundreds of hawks can often be observed in a single day, gliding on billows of air that rise from the Blue Ridge valleys. The Peaks of Otter, near Roanoke, are twin mountains that have been popular with tourists since Jefferson's day; but now the Park Service facilitates your tour with an interpretive visitor center, nature walks and a hiking trail to the summit.

Travel tips and tidbits

The speed limit on the parkway is 45 miles per hour and some stretches are narrow. Should you feel in a hurry, leave the parkway for parallel state and federal highways, where speed limits are higher.

Attractive accommodations on the parkway are available at Peaks of Otter Lodge, 86 miles south of Waynesboro (Box 489, Bedford, VA 24523). Tourist facilities are plentiful in cities and towns along the way. Wintergreen, a private recreation development on 10,000 acres, can be reached from the parkway from the Reeds Gap Exit (between Mileposts 14 and 15) or from U.S. 250 west of Charlottesville. It features many events during the year, such as a Spring Wildflower Symposium, in mid-May; Blue Ridge Nature Festival, in mid-June; and Fall Foliage Festival, in mid-October. (For further information, contact Wintergreen Resort, Wintergreen, VA 22958; call toll-free 1-800-325-2200.)

Where the Ancient River Flows

The New River, one of the few north-flowing rivers in the world, winds and twists froms its origin in North Carolina across Virginia and West Virginia. It is also considered one of the oldest river systems in North America, revealing page after page of earth history. The steep walls of New River Gorge, in fact, expose rocks in some places that date from the Mississippian Age, 330 to 340 million years ago.

The New River is recognized as one of the finest whitewater streams in the East because of challenging rapids in the lower 14-mile section from Thurmond to Fayette Station and because usually reliable waters flow the entire summer season. The 23-mile section from Hinton to Prince offers calmer waters for canoeing and leisurely float trips, but be sure to portage around Sandstone and Brooks Falls!

From the Mountains to the Sea

There are many ways to enjoy the not-so-New River - vistas from overlooks, canoeing and rafting, or taking a train through the New River Gorge.

With such values, it is little wonder New River Gorge was added to the National Park System in 1978—and more, perhaps, that it wasn't included much earlier. The park encompasses 70 miles of river and a total of 50,000 acres. It protects a vast diversity of plants—more than a thousand species.

It is possible to watch spring advance in an almost vertical progression. Leaves are in bud along the river while trees are still bare on the rim of the gorge 700 to 1,400 feet above; spring will come to the top two weeks later than to the river's edge. Consequently spring migration attracts a wide variety of birds in progression, finding diverse vegetation and habitat. Among the first, in late March and early April, are the swallows—of no less than six different species—followed by red-winged blackbirds and phoebes, then by beautiful, songful warblers.

By April's end, each day brings another new species. A dawn-to-dusk birding trip early in May, when migration peaks, may yield as many as 100 different types. By late May most spring migrants have gone farther north, yet during summer more than 70 species can be tallied in a single day.

The place to get oriented is the Canyon Rim Visitor Center near Fayetteville and the New River Gorge Bridge, open all year, or the visitor center at Hinton, open seasonally. The New River Gorge Bridge, arching gracefully

The Canyon Rim Visitor Center located near the New River Gorge Bridge is an important stop for orientation.

across the river, is a showpiece of engineering. Completed in 1977, it is the second highest bridge in the nation, with the world's longest single arch steel span. The bridge reduced a 40-minute drive down narrow mountain roads and across this very old river to less than a minute, which, in our time, is considered "progress."

Many activities originate at Canyon Rim. On summer weekends it's the starting point for bus tours into the gorge. Park rangers regularly lead groups to explore various fascinating aspects of nature and history, like the story of Mary Ingles who in 1755 miraculously found her way back to New River from Ohio after being kidnapped by Indians. The probe of antiquity begins with the age of the river itself, then of humankind—archaelogical surveys show signs of native Americans here 15,000 years ago.

This region figured in the Civil War, with ferries across the New River used by both armies. More recently, coal mining and railroading have been significant factors in culture as well as economy. In 1873 the Chesapeake and Ohio Railway opened the gorge to industrialization. Coal mines were punched into the walls of rock and new towns arose, bearing colorful names such as Alaska, Rush Run, Fire Creek and Red Ash, reflecting hard and dangerous work on a raw frontier.

Even today one special pleasure is the ride through the gorge on Amtrak's "Cardinal," which runs between Chicago and New York. During the summer a park interpreter rides the train from Montgomery to White Sulphur Springs, boarding in the morning and pointing out areas of interest to passengers over the train's PA system, then riding the afternoon westbound "Cardinal" back to the starting point, explaining New River and its coal mining history to Chicago-bound passengers.

From the Mountains to the Sea

This is one of the most unique interpretive services in the national parks, but check to be sure when it is given. As the train passes through tunnels and past abandoned mining towns on the 70-mile trip, the interpreter provides insights on geology, the rise and fall of the coal mining industry, coke making in the valley, and the growing popularity of whitewater rafting and fishing. Some day-trip travelers board the train in the morning, enjoy the commentary through the gorge, spend a two-hour layover at either Hinton or White Sulphur Springs, then ride the afternoon train home.

Autumn colors in October make that month an ideal time to visit. Fall excursion tours on the New River train from the Huntington-Charleston area attract 4,000 people, who enjoy every minute of it.

Travel tips and tidbits

Rafting and kayaking are challenging, popular sports on the New River. From Thurmond, the first few miles downstream are on fairly calm water with small rapids. Then big curling waves and drops begin. Double "Z" describes how to run the most difficult and longest rapid on the river. No matter how skilled the kayaker, it's advisable to join one of the clinics or classes offered by local outfitters. They also feature raft trips, among the most thrilling in the East. At Hinton, the National Park Service offers guided canoe trips

Rafting at Keeney's Creek rapids can be a challenge, and a safe activity on a conducted trip on the New River.

during the summer. Information about raft trips is available from the New River Travel Council, Box 1793, Beckley, WV 25801 (tel. 304-252-2244) or the Fayette County Chamber of Commerce, 214 Main St., Oak Hill, WV 25901.

Hinton emerged as a town when the Chesapeake and Ohio Railway was constructed through the gorge in 1873. To emphasize this railroad heritage, the National Park Service Railroading Weekend is held the third weekend of July. The week-long West Virginia Water Festival is held in August, including a water safety clinic as part of the festivities.

The second Saturday of October is "Bridge Day" in Fayetteville. The New River Gorge Bridge is closed to traffic, and pedestrians are allowed to walk the bridge. Many activities take place including parachute jumps from the bridge!

For two weekends in October the Collis P. Huntington Railroad Society sponsors Fall Foliage Tours through New River Gorge. Often the train is powered by a steam engine, which adds to its appeal as one of the most exciting rides in America. Frequently rafters and kayakers are spotted on the river. When staffing permits, park interpreters provide narration, explaining such features as Sandstone Falls, nine miles north of Hinton, an amazing 1,500 foot wide waterfall. Photo runs are made and one entire car is devoted to the sale of railroad memorabilia. The excursion sells out in advance every year. Make reservations by contacting the Collis P. Huntington Railroad Society at 304-526-5745.

Accommodations in the area include the renowned Greenbrier at White Sulphur Springs, a favorite since the days when spas were in vogue; it's expensive. State parks in the gorge area include Pipestem, Hawks Nest, Babcock, Grandview, Little Beaver and Bluestone. They provide a variety of facilities—lodging, camping, picnicking, swimming, hiking, and nature talks. Several are available all year. For information and reservations telephone 800-CALL-WVA.

Here visitors canoe at the Lackawaxen Pool on the Upper Delaware Scenic and Recreational River.

The Delaware—Zane Grey's Favorite

Here now are two units of the National Park System serving visitors to the upper reaches of another of the East's loveliest rivers—the Delaware, and its forested environs. The river has been much used and exploited, yet still affords recreation and pleasure. Through underground conduits the Delaware supplies half the water needs of metropolitan New York; its upper tributaries have long been dammed, filling reservoirs to store drinking water. Even so, one section or another appeals to fishermen, canoeists, kayakers, birders, artists, followers of old canals and older Indian paths. It was on the banks of the Upper Delaware that Zane Grey began his career as a writer and where, by his own choice, he returned to his final rest.

Delaware Water Gap National Recreation Area, between the Kittatinny ridge in New Jersey and Pocono Mountain Plateau in Pennsylvania, includes about 35 miles of the long, narrow Delaware River Valley. The park was authorized by Congress in 1965, originally projected as part of a proposed major dam and reservoir. Because of strong citizen opposition, however, that dam was never built and basically natural forms of recreation prevail.

The place to begin is at the Delaware Water Gap, a long, mile-wide notch carved by the river, close to Stroudsburg, PA. During the 19th century "the Gap" was a vaunted natural landmark considered almost on a par with Niagara Falls. Stylish hotels capitalized on the view and the entire region was a popular resort destination attracting New York and Philadelphia clientele.

The annual Millbrook Days add life to this 19th century village, one of the many cultural resources in the Delaware Water Gap National Recreation Area.

The National Recreation Area features diverse programs—even summer guided canoe trips on the river. Slateford Farm, near Portland, PA, offers a unique opportunity to learn about slate quarrying. At Millbrook, on New Jersey's Old Mine Road, park personnel demonstrate 19th century crafts. Twelve miles north of Millbrook, Peters Valley Craft Village, near Walpack, enables visitors to learn of contemporary work in fine metals, ceramics, textiles and wood.

The area is excellent for birdwatching, especially during spring migration before leaves are on the trees and again during fall migration. Tremendous flocks of blackbirds spend time in the Delaware Valley in their travels. Spring is colorful with warblers and other perching birds. August marks the beginning of the migration of hawks and eagles.

Waterfalls are plentiful on the Pennsylvania side of the park, and are worth watching in any season. In spring the water is fullest, at maximum flow, and freshest. The summer waterfall ravine is shaded with mountain

The excitement and beauty of the waterfalls add particular interest on the Pennsylvania side of the Delaware Water Gap.

laurel, luxuriant and showy rhododendron, and with hemlock. Dingmans Falls, eight miles south of Milford on Route 209, is one of the choicest spots, with an audiovisual program and exhibits at the visitor center and a pleasant trail through the woods.

The 73-mile stretch of the Upper Delaware Scenic and Recreational River begins a few miles above Port Jervis, NY (while Delaware Water Gap National Recreational Area reaches to a few miles below it). The upper river flows through forested and rolling country between the Poconos of Pennsylvania and the Catskills of New York. This new unit of the National Park System is different than most, since the federal government administers only the river portion while encouraging the two states, their counties and towns to safeguard the forested, farmed and rolling shoreline country.

From Port Jervis, drive north along the river, then across the historic Roebling Bridge to Lackawaxen, on the Pennsylvania side. Here, in relative isolation, Zane Grey began his illustrious writing career. He had been a dentist in New York, but yearned for a literary life. In the big white frame house where he lived with his wife, Grey wrote furiously, even scribbling on plain white paper—though always allowing time for fishing in the stream at hand. He went on to wealth and fame in California, but always regarded the Delaware as home.

He may have gotten his first ideas about Indians here, in the homeland of the ancient Lenape. They were peaceful people who, by the time of the American Revolution, had moved elsewhere. But on a bluff across the river from Lackawaxen another group of Indians, not as peaceful, fought and won the Battle of Minisink in July 1779. A wooded park and historic markers commemorate the engagement between Chief Joseph Brant and his Mohawk warriors and an unfortunate company of colonial militia.

The Upper Delaware is very popular canoe country. Try to plan your trips during midweek; weekends can be crowded, especially on stretches from Narrowsburg south. A choice full-day canoe trip in little spoiled surroundings is the 21-mile run between public access sites located 2 miles north of Equinunk, PA, to Callicoon, NY. The river is generally peaceful and quiet. Your company is likely to include a great blue heron poking its sharp beak for a fish in the shallows or a fisherman wading in hip boots. It takes time to paddle, but the river is the place to forget about time.

The Delaware River has served as an important link in the area's transportation history. The National Park Service-maintained Roebling Bridge was constructed in 1848 as an aqueduct, designed to carry canal boats across the Delaware River, near the mouth of the Lackawaxen. The aqueduct was one of four such structures built by John Roebling for the Delaware and Hudson Canal Company. Roebling later applied the technology he developed here in his design of the Brooklyn Bridge.

Travel tips and tidbits

On the Upper Delaware, all campgrounds, lodgings and restaurants in the river valley are privately owned. The National Park Service operates field offices at Cochecton, NY, and Shohola, PA; an information center in Narrowsburg, NY, and information stations at key public access sites along the river.

On Saturday mornings during summer, park rangers provide basic canoe instructions at Narrowsburg and Ten Mile River access areas. The Information Center on Main Street in Narrowsburg provides guidance on canoeing, as well as other activities and events. If you don't bring your own canoe, you can easily arrange a rental (including drop off and pick up) at one of several liveries. For daily reports on river and boating conditions, call the Information Line at 914-252-7100.

Many accommodations of wide variety are available to Delaware Water Gap visitors in Stroudsburg, East Stroudsburg and scattered throughout the Poconos of Pennsylvania. On the New Jersey side, public campgrounds are located at High Point State Park, Stokes State Forest and Worthington State Forest. All three have excellent hiking paths. The summit of High Point, the highest elevation in New Jersey (1,803 feet), is crowned with a 220-foot obelisk in the style of the Washington Monument. The magnificent view embraces the Delaware River and mountains of three states—New Jersey, Pennsylvania and New York. Old Mine Youth Hostel, at Hainesville, NJ, provides low-cost lodgings to young people and family groups.

Peters Valley Craft Village is a collaboration of skilled craftsmen who live, work and teach on the New Jersey side of the recreation area.

Grey Towers, the family home of Gifford Pinchot, pioneer conservationist and two-time governor of Pennsylvania, is the showpiece of Milford, PA. It is administered by the U.S. Forest Service, which Pinchot once headed. Visitors are invited to free tours of the mansion and grounds.

Mark down on your travel calendar the Peters Valley Crafts Fair the last weekend in July, featuring demonstrations, displays and music at Peters Valley Craft Village; and Millbrook Days the first weekend in October, the annual fall festival with country crafts and home cooking at Millbrook Village.

A Showpiece of Architecture and Landscape Art

Hampton National Historic Site, at Towson, MD, a Baltimore suburb, while not preserving nature in the wild like the other parks on this tour, does represent in its gardens and grounds humankind's harmony with nature. The estate has evolved over the years as an expression of a single family, the Ridgelys, who occupied the mansion for six generations.

You could easily spend an entire day exploring, admiring and contemplating various aspects of horticulture, landscape art, architecture, furniture and decorative arts, all woven into Hampton's history. Before starting, purchase and review a copy of the well-designed "Gardens and Grounds" brochure; more than a guide or walking tour, it shows why visitors for almost 200 years, including Lafayette and Theodore Roosevelt, have enjoyed Hampton.

The Ridgely family owned the Hampton estate from 1745 to 1948, and the farm portion until 1980. The mansion itself, built by Captain Charles Ridgely, was completed in 1790. Later, in the same year, his nephew, Charles Carnan Ridgely, acquired the property. Though active in the political and commercial life of the state (he was governor of Maryland from 1815 to 1818), Charles Carnan Ridgely's greatest interest clearly was focused upon Hampton. He approved extensive landscaping, installing wooden irrigation pipes to convey water from nearby springs.

The parterre gardens, laid out by 1801 on a series of descending terraces, followed a strict geometric design once favored by European aristocracy. With authentic plant materials of the 18th and early 19th centuries, they are the crowning glory of Hampton's gardens and illustrate an important phase of American garden development.

The north lawn design is adapted from the English landscape park, popularized by Britain's famed "Capability" Brown and Humphry Repton—seemingly simple and informal, yet carefully designed to look natural. Many trees on the site are giants of their type, like the cedar of lebanon, a state champion and one of the largest in the country; the saucer magnolia, also a state champion, an innovative hybrid when planted during the 1820's; and the pecan tree, a towering 115 feet, the tallest on the property.

The trees' great size and form complement the Georgian mansion, an outstanding example of American domestic architecture. The elaborate five-part house is built with a large main block connected to east and west wings by "hypens," Palladian style dormer windows, and crowned by an imposing octagonal cupola which dominates the roof line. The urn-shaped finials are, in turn, complemented by a series of more than 40 marble urns which delineate the formal gardens.

The mansion obviously was planned for fashionable entertaining. Furnishings include two large sets of Baltimore-painted furniture (original to Hampton), and an important collection of silver, porcelains and textiles. Portraits represent the work of such notable artists as Thomas Sully, John Hesselius, Charles Willson Peale and Rembrandt Peale.

The story of Hampton National Historic Site unfolds on the walking tours of the grounds and gardens along with the conducted tours of the mansion.

From the mansion, walk around the adjacent Orangerie (a reconstruction of the circa 1825 Greek Revival structure that later burned). Don't miss the circa 1790 outbuildings, including stables, ice house, barns and corn crib, privies, historic garden maintenance buildings and greenhouses; and the Lower House, built in the early 18th century with 18th, 19th and 20th century additions.

Travel tips and tidbits

Take a break at midday in your visit by having lunch at The Tearoom in the mansion. Purchase a copy of the guidebook, illustrated with color and black-and-white photographs, in the Cooperating Association Gift Shop, and choose particular parts of Hampton to explore in the afternoon.

A choice spot for a picnic is Soldiers Delight Natural Environment Area, nearby at Owings Mill. Nature trails in the 1,500-acre park lead to 19th century chrome mines, a restored log cabin, and a scenic overlook.

Assateague—the Last Wild Beach

Drive east to the Atlantic seaboard to the rare fragment of coastal wilderness protected within the boundaries of Assateague Island National Seashore. Flanked by the resort community of Ocean City, MD, to the north and by the Virginia tip of the Delmarva Peninsula to the south, Assateague is a slender barrier island 37 miles long, the largest undeveloped seashore between Massachusetts and North Carolina.

That Assateague continues to exist in its natural state is something of a miracle. For generations it was isolated and out of the way, a lonely, beautiful retreat. As early as 1935 the National Park Service recommended Assateague for special protection, but little happened, and two decades later private ownership seemed destined to dictate its development. In 1962, however, a severe coastal storm damaged everything on the island, rendering the idea of development unfeasible. By Act of Congress in 1965 Assateague became the sixth national seashore.

Assateague is connected by bridges to the mainland at both the northern end from Maryland and southern end from Virginia. Although the national seashore encompasses all of the island, three agencies assist in its administration. Assateague State Park (680 acres), directly across the bridge from mainland Maryland, provides camping and beach facilities. Approximately 15 miles of the Virginia portion form the Chincoteague

The Chincoteague National Wildlife Refuge at the south end provides unmatched opportunities to see shore birds and seabirds.

National Wildlife Refuge, a paradise in autumn and early spring both for enormous flocks of waterfowl and those who love birdlife. The refuge is the wintering ground for ducks, geese and swans, among its 307 species. At the southern portion of the island, called Tom's Cove Hook, the National Park Service maintains a visitor center and recreation area at the end of the road to the beach.

Between the two developed areas, of north and south, lie 22 miles of roadless marsh and beach. Getting from one end of the island to the other takes driving back to the mainland, but covering distance is never the main objective here. What counts most is the perception of Assateague as a fragile barrier island, adjusting to wind, wave, current and storm.

The north end of the island is fascinating with ever-changing sand dunes and washover areas, marsh grasses, pools, nesting terns and skimmers, as well as shore birds. North Beach, administered by the National Park Service just south of the state park, provides camping and recreation facilities. It's a good place from which to explore the central section of the island.

On the Chincoteague Bay side, the ground is higher. In pine woods above the salt meadows and marshes you're likely to see or hear warblers, possibly an owl, and in spring to find a carpet of lady's slippers. To those who look closely, vegetation on the island can prove an endless adventure. On

From the Mountains to the Sea

the dunes, beach grass is the predominant growth, but on higher ground bayberry and other hardy plants thrive. Wildflowers bloom through the growing months, while beach goldenrod may be in bloom past Thanksgiving. It isn't necessary to go far to find variety, considering the island measures only 1/2 to 3½ miles wide.

To enjoy fully the flocks of shore birds, tramp ten miles of wild beach from the parking area at Tom's Cove north through the wildlife refuge. While four-wheel drive vehicles are permitted to run over the sand on a short portion of Tom's Cove Hook and from south of the recreation area at the north beach in Maryland to the Virginia line, the northern 10 miles of beach in the refuge is wilderness undisturbed and unscarred by vehicles. You may also wish to walk the Pony Trail and Wildlife Drive. Look for Whimbrels with their long curved beaks, colorful Ruddy Turnstones, Sanderlings and various sandpipers. Endangered or threatened Piping Plover and Peregrine Falcon nest in Assateague; so do numerous Tern Skimmers, and Oystercatchers. Over 96 species nest in the park and environs.

Nearly all the island beaches can be traversed by foot. Beachcombing is excellent in winter, though rarely good in summer except near the two inlets at either end or after a heavy storm. The shallow bay offers many places to find hardshell clams and blue crabs if you know how to get them. It takes special equipment, such as clam rakes, crab traps or bait lines. Check with a park ranger on where and how to do it best.

The most famous animals on the island are the free-roaming Chincoteague ponies. They're likely to be seen anywhere—and often to appear

The wild ponies of Assateague are the island's best known inhabitants - small, sturdy and shaggy. Careless visitors are injured by bites and kicks.

suddenly. The best way to enjoy them is from a distance. Trying to feed them is definitely a mistake, considering it is apt to lead to injurious bites or painful kicks.

Assateague is enriched by a variety of wildlife, all of which should be treated with respect and a degree of caution. This includes 13 species of reptiles and amphibians, including the threatened loggerhead sea turtle; Japanese Sika deer, a herd grown from a few released by Boy Scouts years ago; the endangered Delmarva fox squirrel, as well as fox, opossum, white-tailed deer, raccoon, rabbit, muskrat and otter.

Islands in the waters of Chincoteague Bay lie within the boundaries of the national seashore. The bay, in fact, should not be overlooked as an attraction. Bring your own canoe and obtain a permit to stay at one or more of the unique canoe-in campsites along the bayside. Short, interpretive canoe trips are given for visitors by the Park Service.

The shallow waters of Assateague's bay side offer excellent waters for canoeing and boating.

Travel tips and tidbits

Conventional two-wheel drive vehicles can travel on the island a distance of 3½ miles from the Maryland bridge and 4 miles from the Assateague Island bridge in Virginia. Four-wheel drive vehicles are subject to a fee permit system, equipment requirements, and restrictions on the use of the 16 miles of beach open to them. For instance, when 18 to 20 pairs of Piping Plovers (a threatened species) successfully fledged young in the summer of 1985 along the southern tip of Assateague, the refuge administration announced it would restrict access annually during nesting season.

Light cartop boats can be launched at mainland ramps and used in most of the shallow bay. Heavier boats are restricted to bay channels or the ocean. Marinas are available in Chincoteague, VA, and Ocean City, MD.

From the Mountains to the Sea

National Park Service visitor centers are located at both ends of the island offering films, naturalist-led walks, evening programs and activities designed specially for children. During summer, naturalists at each center feed creatures in the saltwater aquarium and follow up with a lively discussion. If you bring your canoe, don't miss the chance for a naturalist-led trip on Chincoteague Bay. At the southern tip, the Tom's Cove Hook Visitor Center provides fine wildlife exhibits composed of original art. The guided "Marine Ecology" walk involves active participation—pulling a fishing net to look closely at coastal plants and animals.

At the wildlife refuge, two concession-operated trips help visitors to observe and understand wildlife in its habitat. The Safari Trip, operating in the morning, carries up to 40 passengers in a screened vehicle along the 7½-mile service road. A guide interprets wildlife, which may include nesting Peregrine Falcon. In early evening, a cruise boat, the **Osprey**, leaves from the refuge for a tour around Assateague Channel. Obtain information about these two trips, and purchase tickets for them, at the Refuge Visitor Center.

If you're camping, Assateague State Park provides 311 modern sites on hardtop loop roads, as well as protected beach, bathhouse and food service. North Beach, just below the state park, offers two primitive family campgrounds and lifeguard protection for swimmers. Three backcountry hike-in campsites are located behind the primary dune, and four canoe-in or hike-in campsites are located on the bay side; these are quite primitive and all water and shelter must be packed in. On the Virginia side, all camping must be in commercial facilities on nearby Chincoteague Island. Come prepared with repellant in summer to cope with mosquitoes and green-headed flies.

Many beach activities are popular at Assateague— swimming, shell collecting, surf fishing, or taking a seashore walk with a park ranger.

Noncampers have the choice of many motels at Ocean City, MD or Chincoteague, VA. Each town is about 20 minutes from Assateague beaches; reservations are recommended in summer. At Chincoteague fishing boats may be rented. There are delightful "bed and breakfast" spots and excellent restaurants. For canoe rentals inquire at the National Seashore. The National Aeronautics and Space Administration maintains a space and tracking station at Wallops Island, which you see before crossing the causeway to reach Chincoteague Island. On your right the NASA museum interprets the space program with rockets and other missiles and equipment.

Mark these events in your travel calendar: Waterfowl Decoy Shows in Chincoteague on Easter weekend, in Ocean City on the last weekend in April and in Salisbury on the first weekend in October; Pony Penning Week, the annual roundup and auction of the celebrated ponies by Chincoteague "cowboys," held the last Wednesday and Thursday in July; Waterfowl Week, when the refuge opens the 7½-mile service road to visitors (weather conditions permitting) from the Saturday prior to Thanksgiving to the Sunday following Thanksgiving.

The Pinelands—A Different Kind of Park

Located within 50 miles of Philadelphia and 100 miles of New York City, Pinelands National Reserve was established to preserve and enhance the distinctive tract of 1,100,000 acres in southern New Jersey, a region once derided as the "pine barrens." It's almost at the backdoor of Atlantic City, from which you can easily reach the Pinelands and discover much to enjoy in the complex of pine-oak forest, cedar swamps and streams.

The Reserve is a different kind of national park, based on federal coordination rather than ownership. Where Assateague was shown to be infeasible for building, three-fifths of the Pinelands is privately owned, with farms, small villages and towns dotting the area. They are underlain by a natural 17 trillion gallon aquifer, a layer of ground water in the sand. This weighed strongly in Congressional action to designate this unit of the National Park System in 1978.

Pinelands National Reserve comprises one of the largest parcels of open space on the Mid-Atlantic coast. The heart of the area, Wharton State Forest, near Atsion, covers more than 100,000 acres; it is the largest tract of state park and forest land in New Jersey. Though there are no National Park Service facilities, visitors may tour Batsto Mansion, mills, and workers homes in the restored 18th century iron-making community within the state forest. It makes a good starting point for hiking, camping and canoeing in little disturbed natural settings.

From the Mountains to the Sea

Some 400 miles of sand roads, though mostly unmarked, are well suited for naturalist exploration and enjoyment of sphagnum moss, wild orchids, the vast pigmy pine "plains," blueberries and cranberries. Try a section of the 40-mile Batona Trail, which starts at Batsto and runs north to New Lebanon State Forest. Canoeing is choice on four of south New Jersey's popular streams winding through the wilderness. Keep a sharp eye for insect eating plants, deer, squirrel, beaver and raccoon.

Travel tips and tidbits

A Cranberry Festival is held in October at Chatsworth, a village on Rt. 563 in the heart of the pines. Whitesbog, near Fort Dix, hosts a Blueberry Festival in June.

Flooded cedar swamps of characteristic tea-colored water are seen adjacent to scenic rivers in the Pinelands National Reserve.

Cranberry farming operations continue in the Pinelands, with the cranberry harvest being a colorful fall event.

Be sure to visit nearby Brigantine National Wildlife Refuge at Oceanville on the coast (about 12 miles north of Atlantic City). Pick up a copy of the self-guiding tour leaflet showing the way to nature trails and observation blinds. Birdwatching is tops during spring and fall migrations. Smithville, just north of Oceanville, is a popular commercial version of an 18th century New Jersey community with specialty shops and a variety of dining rooms. Craft demonstrations are given mid-June to Labor Day.

Barnegat National Wildlife Refuge is easy to reach by going 20 miles north on the Garden State Parkway (Rt. 9) to Manahawkin near the coast. Then, from there for a thrilling sight, continue east across the causeway to Ship Bottom, then north on Long Beach Island to Barnegat Lighthouse—"Grand Old Champion of the Tides." Climb to the top of the lighthouse, 217 steps above the base, for a superlative view of Barnegat Shoals, the scene of more than 200 shipwrecks. Make the most of the unspoiled primitive surroundings in Barnegat Lighthouse State Park.

Park ranger naturalists in Shenandoah National Park help you to explore the world of nature.

From the Mountains to the Sea

Park Information

Assateague Island National Seashore
Rt. 2, Box 294, Berlin, MD 21811
(301) 641-1441

Seashore Visitor Center—8 miles south of Ocean City, MD via Rt. 50 West and Rt. 611 South.

Tom's Cove Visitor Center—4 miles east of Chincoteague, VA via Beach Road.

Visitor Center Hours 8:30—5:00

Delaware Water Gap NRA
Bushkill, PA 18324
(717) 588-6637

Dingman's Falls Visitor Center—One mile west on Highway 209 near Dingman's Ferry, PA.

Visitor Center hours 9:00—5:00 late April through October.

Kittatinny Point Visitor Center—The first exit east of Interstate 80, Delaware River toll bridge in New Jersey.

Visitor Center hours 9:00—5:00 Mid-April through October; 9:00—4:00 weekends remainder of year.

Hampton National Historic Site
535 Hampton Lane
Towson, MD 21204
(301) 823-7054

Visitor Center—The park is accessible from the Baltimore Beltway (I-695) via exits 27 and 28 north. Public transportation from Baltimore serves the Towson area within a mile of the park. In Towson, take Dulaney Valley Road (Md. 146) north across the Beltway and immediately turn right on Hampton Lane, which leads to the park. This is a dangerous intersection; be careful not to enter the Beltway ramps located adjacent to Hampton Lane.

Visitor Center hours Mon.—Sat. 11:00—4:30; Sun. 1:00—4:30. Advanced notices for groups of ten or more are requested.

New River Gorge National River
P.O. Box 1189
Oak Hill, WV 25901
(304) 465-0508

Canyon Rim Visitor Center—Located on U.S. 19 approximately two miles north of Fayetteville, West Virginia (just North of the New River Gorge Bridge).

Hinton Visitor Center—Located on the Rt. 20 bypass just South of Hinton, West Virginia (open summers only).

Pinelands National Reserve
P.O. Box 7
New Lisbon, NJ 08064
(609) 894-9342

Visitor Center—Pinelands National Reserve has no visitor center; however, the Batsto Visitor Center in the Pine Barrens in Wharton State Forest, Washington Township, Burlington County, provides visitor services. Telephone number (609) 561-0024. Follow Route 30E from Philadelphia, to 542E to Hammonton, NJ.

Visitor Center hours 10:00—4:00 at Batsto Visitor Center in the Pine Barrens in Wharton State Forest

Shenandoah National Park
Rt. 4, Box 292
Luray, VA 22835
(703) 999-2243

Visitor Center—Mile 4.6 Dickey Ridge Visitor Center winter/summer
Mile 51 Byrd Visitor Center winter/summer

Visitor Center hours 9:00—5:00

Upper Delaware Scenic & Recreational River
P.O. Box C
Narrowsburg, NY 12764
(717) 729-7134

Visitor Center—Located at Arts Center Building, Main Street, Narrowsburg, NY

Visitor Center hours 9:00—4:30

An Assateague seashore conducted walk with a park ranger is always a "discovery experience".

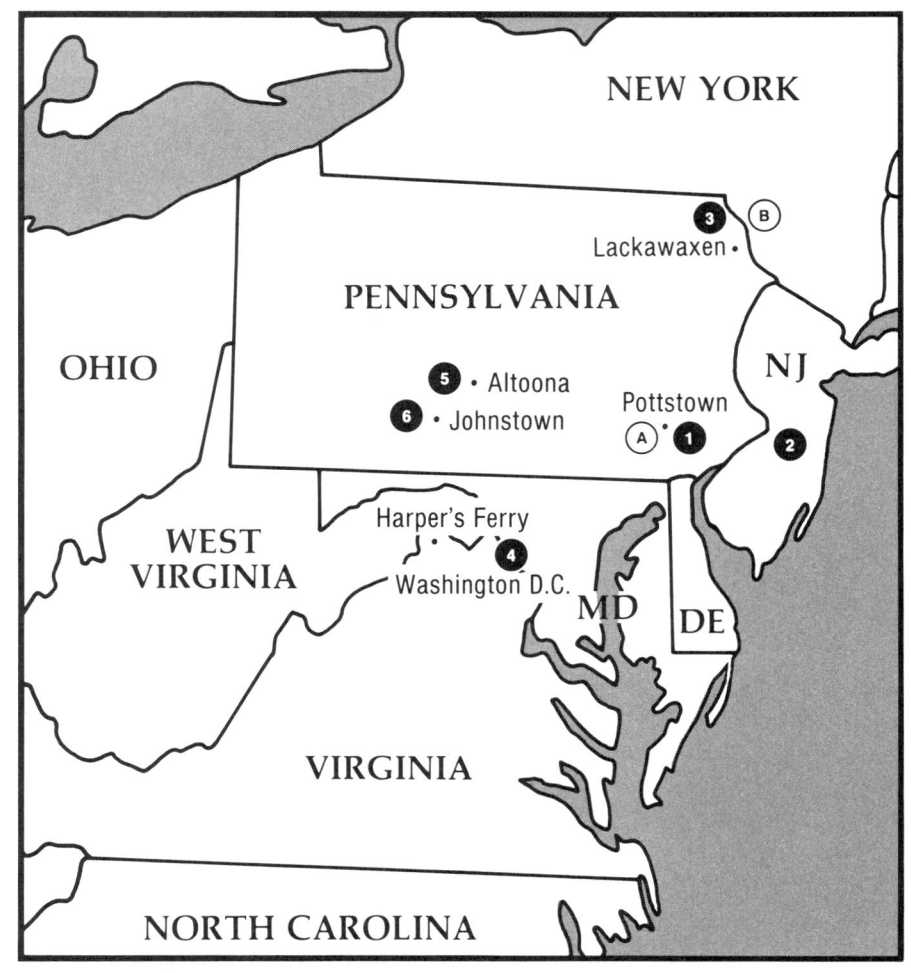

Tour Three
1. Hopewell Furnace National Historic Site
2. Batsto State Historic Site
3. Roebling Bridge
4. Chesapeake and Ohio Canal National Historical Park
5. Allegheny Portage Railroad National Historic Site
6. Johnstown Flood National Memorial

Additional Sights
Ⓐ French Creek State Park
Ⓑ Minisink Ford

Tour Three

In the Age of Crafts
A Tour of Industry and Engineering

The American economy and culture in the early years of settlement were agrarian, rural-based, and from the beginning craft-workers produced implements that people needed. Production and demand developed into a process that culminated in the Industrial Age. The glasshouse at Jamestown, in fact, is assumed to represent the country's first factory. The replica today provides the setting for demonstrating the process of 17th century glassblowing—one of many ways national parks recount the emergence of manufacture and the skills associated with it.

In due course, a variety of items were produced, mostly by hand at first, then by simple machines which evolved into more sophisticated devices with time. Raw materials were extracted from the earth. Trade grew; so did transportation, as civilization moved west. American life was continually endowed with more convenience, and with more complexity as well.

Benjamin Franklin—printer, publisher and inventive genius—doubtless would be thunderstruck by our modern system of communication. On the other hand, he chose deliberately to build his house in the court off Market

In the Age of Crafts

Street in Philadelphia to be in the midst of the friends of his youth. His immediate neighbors were artisans, craftsmen and shopkeepers, whom he called "leather apron men."

In our "high-tech" age more and more people are fascinated by ways of the past. Men and women alike do needlepoint and weaving, collect and make their own muzzle-loading rifles, furniture and all manner of challenging memorabilia. A look back at the hand-tooling of simpler days is like a refresher course in the values of self-sufficiency and in the pride of the craft.

Parks on this tour are grouped by the industries they represent. Hopewell Furnace National Historic Site, near Birdsboro, PA, is the finest surviving example of thousands of charcoal ironworks that once thrived in eastern United States. It was an important source of cannon, shot, and shell for Continental forces during the American Revolution. The Batsto Iron Works, in Wharton State Forest, encompassed by Pinelands National Reserve, NJ, was still another producer of desperately needed iron materials. Hopewell and Batsto represent the old "iron plantations" that were more than factories—they were industrial communities.

As the country grew, improved transportation became essential. During the 19th century, canals and railroads answered the demand for speed and convenience. Pennsylvania alone built 1,200 miles of canal and one of the prime remembrances of that era is preserved as part of the Upper Delaware Scenic and Recreational River. That is the Delaware Aqueduct, or the "Roebling Bridge," named for its designer, John A. Roebling, known today for his later masterpiece of engineering design, the Brooklyn Bridge.

Still another national park unit, the Chesapeake and Ohio Canal National Historical Park, preserves one of the longest, least-altered canals built in the pre-railroad era. Today's visitor can sample the past on a mule-drawn boat trip from either Georgetown, at the western edge of Washington, DC, or from Potomac, MD.

Getting canal boats over the steep mountains of western Pennsylvania was an engineering challenge, answered for a time by a technological marvel—an inclined plane railway system, at Allegheny Portage Railroad National Historic Site, outside Cresson, PA. However, progress has its price, as evidenced at Johnstown Flood National Memorial, a few miles southwest of Cresson. In the spring of 1889, the South Fork Dam (built to supply water to the Pennsylvania Canal), collapsed under the pressure of heavy rains, leading to the monumental Johnstown Flood.

The parks on this tour represent high spots in the saga of industry and engineering ingenuity, but there are others as well in the Mid-Atlantic

Region. Be on the lookout for them. Notice the relationship between natural resources—water, soil, timber, iron, coal—and the advance of civilization.

Hopewell and Batsto—Iron Villages

Hopewell Furnace National Historic Site, five miles south of Birdsboro, PA, is the most completely restored of all the old "iron plantations," representative of hundreds that once existed in Pennsylvania alone. A visit to Hopewell today is an exploration of industrial, cultural, and social history, a closeup of an industrial community of 150 years ago.

Hopewell was built in 1771 on the headwaters of French Creek, a few short years before the American Revolution. When war came, Mark Bird, the ironmaster, and the community turned to serving the Continental forces. At his own expense, Bird outfitted troops and served as a colonel of militia. As deputy quartermaster general, he shipped large quantities of supplies to General George Washington at Valley Forge (23 miles away, and which you can easily visit on the same trip).

Hopewell Furnace is one of the finest examples of a rural American 19th century ironmaking village.

75

In the Age of Crafts

The peak of prosperity was reached at Hopewell in the decades of 1820-1840. Products such as stove parts, kettles, pots, machine castings and pig iron flowed from the furnace. Though declining from its economic peak, Hopewell continued to produce iron until 1883, when newer production methods had clearly made it obsolete.

The area is distinguished as the first industrial site to be included in the National Park System. You can readily see how raw materials (iron ore, limestone, and hardwood forests for charcoal) were all available close at hand. Exhibits and illustrated programs at the visitor center, and the walking tour, interpret every step of the process of producing molded or cast iron products and the lives of the people who made the process work. With imagination you can picture the scene when the furnace was in full blast: the furnace stack roaring, the water wheel clanking, woodcutters chopping hardwood billets to feed the hearths in the woods, the molders utilizing sand and wooden patterns to cast intricate and difficult designs in their stove plates. It's all here in the "Big House" (the Ironmaster's mansion), blacksmith shop, charcoal house, furnace, water wheel, bridge house, barn, tenant homes and company store. It was a way of life, of 12-hour shifts, in the noisy and smoky furnace, with scant time for play and pleasure in the natural environs.

In the cast house, skilled Hopewell molders produced parts for over 80,000 stoves before the furnace reverted solely to pig iron production.

There is even a vestige of the old wagon road that once reached from Reading to Valley Forge. It was the growing system of roads, and later canals and railroads, that enabled Hopewell to distribute its products. The barn tells a story of transportation, with a variety of wagons and carriages— two-wheel dump cart, freight wagon, charcoal wagon and one-horse chaise— and yes, horses and mules, too!

Hopewell and the other ironmaking villages ultimately became the victims of time and technology. The old system of charcoal smelting was replaced by new techniques utilizing coal and heated air blasts. Factories were closer to urban markets than were the old "iron plantations" in the woods.

Still, the living history program during summer rekindles the sense of times past. Interpreters in period dress conduct the activities that kept the furnace operating and the normal everyday comings and goings of the village, from charcoal making to bread baking.

Early residents of Batsto Village mined bog-iron from the banks of streams and bogs in this unique region—the New Jersey Pinelands.

Batsto Village, in Pinelands National Reserve, recounts another page in the same chapter of industrial history. Because of bog iron found in the vicinity, the Batsto Iron Works was established here in 1766. During the Revolutionary War Batsto, like Hopewell, was an important source of supplies for the Americans; Batsto, in fact, was attacked by British forces.

Colonial iron villages had practical reason for their patriotism. Though American pig iron commanded a high price in Britain, the Iron Act of 1750 limited the American industry to producing pig and bar iron that could be reworked by British forges into finished products, then exported to the colonies. Though the Act was often evaded, it led many ironmasters to oppose all imperial regulations.

In the Age of Crafts

Following the American Revolution, Batsto prospered. It thrived briefly during the early 19th century as an iron and glassmaking community, but by 1848 its day was done; the old furnaces were shut for the last time. In 1876 the land was purchased by Joseph Wharton, whose immense estate totaled nearly 100,000 acres. In 1954 this became the state forest bearing his name. The scene remains generally undisturbed. The general store, gristmill, blacksmith shop, wheelwright shop, sawmill and workers' houses are still in place, open to visitors on guided tours during summer.

Travel tips and tidbits

The roots of the iron industry go back almost to the beginning of English settlement. In 1621, upriver from Jamestown, VA, the first recorded attempt was made to produce iron. Twenty-five years later (1646) a more successful ironworks was established at Saugus, MA. A careful reconstruction is now contained in Saugus Iron Works National Historical Site. Keep it in mind for some future trip to New England.

Other ironmaking sites well worth visiting in Pennsylvania include: Caledonia Furnace, Caledonia State Park, Fayetteville; Cornwall Furnace, Cornwall; Greenwood Furnace, Greenwood Furnace State Park; Pine Grove Furnace, Pine Grove State Park, Gardners; and Scranton Furnaces, Scranton.

Hopewell, however, is the most complete of all, and not by accident. In 1935, the federal government purchased the Hopewell property from Mrs. Louise Clingan Brooke, whose family had owned it for 135 years. The historic value was not recognized—the idea actually was to develop a recreation demonstration area using Civilian Conservation Corps labor. Even though neglect and the elements had taken their toll, a number of furnace structures were still standing and led to the arrival on the scene of Roy Appleman, a National Park Service historian. He identified Hopewell's significance; largely through his efforts, the national historic site was established in 1938. Restoration began in earnest in the 1950s with 19th century construction methods, including beams hewn by hand and joined with wooden dowels.

Hopewell lies 10 miles from the Morgantown interchange of the Pennsylvania Turnpike. French Creek State Park, immediately adjacent, once part of the Hopewell property, provides facilities for camping, picnicking and swimming.

The Canal in its Heyday

By the 1820s canal fever hit America. A spreading web of canals carried settlers and supplies to the western frontier, returning products of forests, mines and farms to eastern cities. Canals were costly to build, but they

The Roebling "Bridge" is in reality an aqueduct which carried the Delaware and Hudson Canal across the Delaware River.

made transportation smooth and dependable. Locks and aqueducts conveyed the canal over a stream or deep depression. Mules furnished the main source of power, pulling the canal boats while walking sure-footed along the towpath.

Much of Pennsylvania's canal system was built along the Delaware River or on streams feeding into or flowing from it. The Delaware and Hudson Canal, extending from Honesdale, PA, to Kingston, NY, was designed to facilitate the transport of anthracite to New York City. It included a key link, the Roebling Bridge, which lies within the Upper Delaware Scenic and Recreational River (covered also in Tour II).

The Roebling Bridge was built in response to a critical need. The first 25 miles of the Delaware and Hudson Canal originally followed the Lackawaxen River to its junction with the Delaware at Minisink Ford. Canal boats, however, would occasionally collide with timber rafts coming down the main river. Inventiveness thus led to the decision to "build the canal above the water" with a suspension aqueduct.

John A. Roebling, a young engineer with experience in western Pennsylvania, was engaged to design the span. When it was completed in 1848, could anyone have foreseen that he would become the architect of the most famous bridge in the world—the Brooklyn Bridge?

The Roebling Bridge, America's oldest wire suspension bridge, is supported by three imposing stone buttresses and extends 535 feet across the Delaware. It included a long trough with two thick sides, wide and deep enough to hold a canal boat in flowing water. An entire family would live on board and operate the canal boat, sluicing over the Delaware on the trip of about 10 days from Honesdale to Kingston.

In its heyday of the 1850s, the canal transported a million tons of cargo a year. Before the turn of the century, however, the advent of railroading

In the Age of Crafts

The canal boat, "Georgetown," on the C&O Canal—which endures as a national historical park—a 185 mile pathway to history, nature, and recreation.

spelled its doom. Today, luckily the traveler can piece the scene together at the Roebling Bridge and the ruins of stonework, locks and overgrown towpaths between Minisink Ford and Port Jervis, NY.

Still another unit of the National Park system, the Chesapeake and Ohio Canal National Historical Park, MD, preserves one of the longest, least altered of canals built in the pre-railroad age. At its peak, during the 1870s, about 500 boats navigated the 185 miles from Cumberland, in western Maryland, to Georgetown, the western edge of Washington, DC, loaded with coal, flour, grain and lumber. Today's visitors can sample the past on a mule-drawn boat trip from either Georgetown or from historic Great Falls Tavern in Potomac, MD; during the 1½-hour trip, guides in period dress describe daily life and perform music of the canal era.

Once aboard the "Georgetown," park rangers guide visitors through a part of the nation's capital that many people never see—the part dug by Irish immigrants 150 years ago. The "Georgetown," christened in 1982, is a 90-foot by 14-foot fiberglas-and-wood replica of an original boat. Though it must pass under a bridge with a clearance of three feet, it manages through the engineering magic of locks.

The approach to each of the two locks on the upstream trip is heralded by the sound of a horn, blown by the boatman at the tiller, to warn the locktender of the boat's approach. Once in the lock, boatman and locktender close the lock gates to the rear of the boat. Then using a heavy iron wrench, the boatman opens paddles on the lock gates to the front of the boat, allowing water to flow into the lock. As the water fills the lock, the boat rises to the new water level and the upstream gates are opened.

Two mules plod patiently along the towpath, pulling the "Georgetown" at about four miles an hour, while two mule drivers walk with them, reins in hand. Passengers are treated to stories of barge life, including the fate of the boatman's children, whose job it was to tend the mules, rain or shine, from April to October.

The Chesapeake and Ohio Canal was never profitable. It competed with the Baltimore and Ohio Railroad, but unsuccessfully, and use was discontinued in 1924. It has since been known as "one of the loveliest failures in all of history." The towpath of the entire canal makes for excellent hiking or bicycling. Along the way, 500 structures remain to represent the canal era, when each boat was raised and lowered through 75 locks.

An 1880 view of a loaded canal boat coming downstream into the Conococheague Aqueduct, at the C&O Canal at Williamsport, Maryland.

Travel tips and tidbits

A very pleasant drive to see the Roebling Bridge leads from Port Jervis, NY, along the Delaware River. Pull off at the overlook where the road climbs high above the Upper Delaware to observe the contour of the river and bordering forested hills. On a summer weekend the water likely will be covered by hundreds of canoes moving downstream.

Stop for a snack or refreshment at the Minisink Inn, perched on a cliffside, at the Minisink Ford next to the Roebling Bridge. You can take a leisurely walk across the bridge into Lackawaxen, where Zane Grey lived and is buried. The bridge for several years was closed to auto traffic but has been reopened following repair and reinforcement. On the Pennsylvania side, you can drive to Shohola, a resort in the old railroad days, and then to Milford; or drive north to Honesdale, where the Delaware and Hudson Canal began.

In the Age of Crafts

Along the upper towpath on the Chesapeake and Ohio Canal, the National Park Service has installed a series of simple campsites; these are 10 miles apart, from Dam 3, opposite Harpers Ferry, WV, to Cumberland. The Kiwanis Youth Hostel, near Harpers Ferry, provides simple, inexpensive accommodations for hikers and bicyclists. It is close to mile 58 on the canal, where the Appalachian Trail crosses the Potomic River.

Congress in 1977 officially dedicated the Chesapeake and Ohio Canal National Historical Park to William O. Douglas, who had retired two years earlier as a justice of the Supreme Court, "in grateful recognition of his long-outstanding service as a prominent American conservationist and for his efforts to preserve and protect the canal and towpath from development." In 1954 Justice Douglas described the canal and its environment as a long stretch of quiet and peace "not yet marred by the roar of wheels and sound of horns." He then led a group of hikers along the full length of the towpath, 185 miles from Cumberland to Washington, to prove his point.

Portaging Barges over the Mountain

A technological feat and engineering marvel in its own day, the Allegheny Portage Railroad even now stands as one of the most unusual means of overland transportation ever conceived. This phenomenal inclined plane railway system was devised to haul canal boats over the steep Allegheny Mountains between Hollidaysburg and Johnstown in western Pennsylvania. While the Allegheny Portage Railroad connected with the Pennsylvania Canal at either end, it was all railroad for 36 miles—no railroad-canal combination. The 36-mile railroad facilitated continuous transportation between Philadelphia and Pittsburgh, one of the major routes in westward expansion.

Primitive rail tracks have been reconstructed on a level section of the Allegheny Portage Railroad near Cresson, Pennsylvania.

Allegheny Portage Railroad National Historic Site, PA, preserves and interprets this brief chapter in industrial and engineering development. The impressive stone Lemon House has been a prominent landmark since 1834, shortly after completion of the Portage Railroad, first as a tavern and eatery, now as the visitor center of the park.

At first, cargo was unloaded from barges on one side of the mountain, hauled across on flatbed railroad cars, via inclined planes and level stretches, then reloaded onto other barges. But improvements were constantly made. Steam locomotives, for instance, replaced horses as portage power. John A. Roebling, the engineering wizard, suggested substituting wire for hemp ropes (which often broke and were a constant source of trouble) to pull the cars. Finally, canal boats were built in three or four completely watertight sections that could be disassembled, safely hoisted over the mountain, put back together and set afloat in the canal on the other side. All this was done without disturbing the family's arrangements for cooking, sleeping and daily activity.

Though ingenious as an engineering experiment, the Portage Railroad lasted only 20 years. Its day was done in 1854 when railroading introduced big powerful locomotives and the new Horseshoe Curve route across the mountains.

The park preserves buildings and structures, including four of the 10 inclined planes, stone culverts, foundations of the engine house, and the

A wayside sign helps to explain the scene and the stationary steam engines which raised and lowered rail cars on the Allegheny Portage Railroad.

In the Age of Crafts

Skew Arch Bridge, so named because it had to be skewed, or twisted, at an angle over the railroad. Various trails trace the old route, allowing a perception of what Charles Dickens felt during his 1842 trip. "Occasionally the rails are laid upon the extreme verge of a giddy precipice," he wrote, "and looking from the carriage window, the traveler gazes sheer down without a stone or scrap of fence between into the mountain depths below." Nonetheless, Dickens felt that all proper precautions were taken and the trip was "not to be dreaded for its dangers."

There were, however, dangers of another type in the region, and they went completely unrecognized. The South Fork Dam and Western Reservoir, built to supply water during dry spells for the Johnstown Canal Basin, looked foolproof when they were completed in 1853. Their proponents, in fact, could proudly point to one of the largest earthen dams in the world and one of the largest artificial lakes in the nation.

Ironically, even while the dam was being completed, the canal system approached obsolescence. The reservoir was abandoned and left to deteriorate for two decades. In 1879 a group of Pittsburgh industrialists purchased the site, repaired the dam (but not too efficiently, as it turned out), and established an exclusive resort development. They enjoyed fishing, sailing and had two excursion steamers cruising the reservoir, which they called Lake Conemaugh.

All went well until heavy rains fell in the spring of 1889. The dam burst under pressure. The lake emptied in 40 minutes, releasing a wall of water down the Little Conemaugh Valley directly into Johnstown. The monu-

The south abutment of the South Fork Dam at Johnstown Flood National Memorial is an excellent viewpoint from which to observe the remains of the dam which failed on May 31, 1889.

mental Johnstown Flood virtually destroyed the city, leaving in its wake a human death toll of 2,209 and millions of dollars of property damage.

Johnstown Flood National Memorial preserves remnants of the old dam, 12 miles north of the city of Johnstown, PA. The visitor center features a model of the dam and lake and displays on events leading to the tragic flood. On the three-mile loop drive you can trace almost the entire boundary of Lake Conemaugh while passing the 1889 clubhouse and some of the summer cottages. Walk the South Abutment Trail to see the two worn abutments, all that remain of the great earthen dam. "Our misery is the work of man," said someone in Johnstown following the flood.

Travel tips and tidbits

Points of interest are not centralized, but scattered over an extended, rather hilly terrain. Allow plenty of time for driving and walking. Dress informally and appropriately for terrain and weather. Trails in both parks—Allegheny Portage and Johnstown Flood—offer choice opportunities for nature observation. Warblers, grosbeaks, buntings, finches and wrens are often seen.

Do not confuse Johnstown Flood National Memorial with the Johnstown Flood Museum. The museum depicts the history of the city, including floods of 1889, 1936 and 1977. Grandview Cemetery in Johnstown contains the "Unknown Plot," where 777 unidentified victims of the '89 flood are buried under blank headstones.

Neither should you confuse Allegheny Portage with the Railroaders Memorial Museum in nearby Altoona. That museum recalls the birth of the town in 1849, as the base of operations for building the first railroad over the Alleghenies. Don't miss the drive to Horseshoe Curve, the engineering masterpiece in pioneer railroading, five miles west of Altoona. You can see the railroad bed embankment from the parking area, but not the entire embankment of the curve. You must climb up 110 stone steps to actually be in the Horseshoe Curve, see the tracks and any trains going across. Even when climbing up into the curve you do not get to see the full extent due to heavy vegetation, especially in the late spring, summer and early fall months.

Accommodations are extensive and varied in both Altoona and Johnstown. In Ebensburg, the Noon-Collins Inn provides good accommodations and food (814-472-4311). It is a contemporary of the Lemon House and much like it in appearance.

Historic craft demonstrations are given every weekend at Allegheny Portage Railroad from mid-June through Labor Day.

In the Age of Crafts

Park Information

Allegheny Portage Railroad National Historic Site
P.O. Box 247
Cresson, PA 16630
(814) 886-8176

Visitor Center—Lemon House located 1 mile east of Summit Exit on U.S. Route 22.

Visitor Center hours 8:30—5:00 daily (extended hours in summer)

Batsto State Park
Pinelands National Reserve
P.O. Box 7
New Lisbon, New Jersey 08064
(609) 894-9342

Visitor Center—The Batsto Visitor Center In the Pine Barrens in Wharton State Forest, Washington Township, Burlington, County, provides visitor services. Telephone number 609-561-0024. Follow Route 30E from Philadelphia, to 542E to Hammonton, NJ

Visitor Center hours 10:00—4:00 at Batsto Visitor Center in the Pine Barrens in Wharton State Forest

Chesapeake and Ohio Canal National Historical Park
Ferry Hill House (Headquarters)
Box 4
Sharpsburg, MD 21782
(301) 739-4200

Visitor Center—Great Valls Canal Tavern (Main Visitor Center)(boat rides)
11710 MacArthur Boulevard
Potomac, MD 20854
Telephone: 301-299-3614
Visitor Center hours 9:00—5:00

Visitor Center—Georgetown Visitor Center (for boat rides)
Foundry Mall
1055 Thomas Jefferson Street, NW
Washington, DC 20007
(202) 472-6685

Visitor Center hours 11:00—5:00

Visitor Center—Western Maryland Station Visitor Center
Canal Street
Cumberland, MD 21502
(301) 722-8226

Visitor Center hours 11:00—5:00

Hopewell Furnace National Historical Site
R.D. 1 Box 441
Elverson, PA 19520
(215) 582-8773

Visitor Center—Located 5 miles South of Birdsboro on State Highway #345. From the Morgantown exchange the Pennsylvania Turnpike exit left (south) ¼ miles on route 10 then turn left (east) on Route 23 for five miles turn left (north) on Route 345 for 4 miles.

Visitor Center hours 9:00—5:00 (Closed Christmas & New Years)

Johnstown Flood National Monument
c/o ALPO
P.O. Box 247
Cresson, PA 16630
(814) 886-8176

Visitor Center—Located one mile east of Sidman Exit (PA 869) on U.S. Route 219.

Visitor Center hours 8:30—5:00 (daily in summer)

Roebling Bridge
Upper Delaware Scenic & Recreational River
P.O. Box C
Narrowsburg, NY 12764
(717) 729-7134

Visitor Center—Located Arts Center Building, Main Street, Narrowsburg, NY

Visitor Center hours 9:00—4:30

At Hopewell Furnace you may see a skilled carpenter repairing the spokes on a Conestoga wagon wheel. By 1776, these hand-made wagons were one of the important overland vehicles in the country. Preservation and restoration work by 20th century National Park Service craftsmen assure the survival of these historic objects. Today, Conestogas may be seen in several parks; Hopewell Furnace, Fort Necessity and Valley Forge.

Tour Four
1. Gettysburg National Military Park Military Park
2. Antietam National Battlefield
3. Manassas National Battlefield Park
4. Fredericksburg National Military Park
5. Richmond National Battlefield Park
6. Petersburg National Battlefield
7. Appomattox Court House National Historical Park

Additional Sights
A. Harpers Ferry National Historical Park
B. Clara Barton National Historic Site
C. Prince William Forest Park
D. Maggie L. Walker National Historic Site

Tour Four

Hallowed Grounds
A Tour of Civil War Scenes

It was the war that divided the nation, that spread destruction and death across the land, inspired heroism and sacrifice, ended slavery on this continent, and brought immortality to Abraham Lincoln in his pursuit of victory without vengeance and of peace to reunite the people.

The Civil War, despite the passing of time, has lost none of its fascination. Modes of warfare have changed, yet military experts continue to study and debate the strategies and tatics of Grant and Lee and their lieutenants. Scholars from all over the world come to the battlefield parks to learn something new by retracing history.

The earliest of these battlefield parks, incidentally, were established in the 1870's in response to the influence of Civil War veterans, determined as private citizens to memorialize their fallen comrades. It is impossible, indeed, to visit a battlefield park without being moved; surely the country is richer for what has been saved.

Hallowed Grounds

Civil War engagements were fought in many parts of the country, yet virtually from the beginning to the end, fighting raged in the Mid-Atlantic states of Virginia, Maryland and Pennsylvania. Union forces sought to capture Richmond, the Confederate capital, while the Confederates fought to invade Washington, DC, and very nearly succeeded.

Of more than 2,000 land engagements during the war, Gettysburg ranks first in the memory of the nation. Thus, it is the starting point of this tour. From there the route leads south into Maryland, a state which had strong ties to both sides and was sharply divided. It became a major battleground, as evidenced by the Battle of Antietam, the bloodiest single day of the Civil War. Monocacy National Battlefield, MD, even closer to Washington, preserves a vital link in Union efforts to block a Confederate thrust aimed at the national capital.

This tour leads to the site of the first major land battle of the war, fought near Manassas, VA, only 26 miles southwest of Washington, DC. It was an opening test of strength between the two armies, but thirteen months later they returned for the fierce Battle of Second Manassas, that cleared the way for Lee's invasion of Maryland. Continuing south, no other area of comparable size on the American continent has witnessed such heavy and continuous fighting as Fredericksburg and its environs—four major Civil War engagements within a 17-mile radius.

Each of these battlefield parks takes time and patience to appreciate fully. Allow for it in your planning; reading in advance will help considerably. Presently you'll understand the Union battle cry, "On to Richmond," and how to trace the seven military drives hurled at that once beleaguered city. Due south of Richmond, Petersburg was the scene of 10 months of grim siege warfare. With further resistance clearly futile, the end came at last with Lee's surrender to Grant at Appomattox Court House, VA, now restored to present a touching and impressive picture of that day.

The battlefield parks on this itinerary unquestionably rank among the country's foremost military shrines. They recount more than a record of victories and defeats on given dates, but the story of people, people of all kinds, how they lived, worked, fought, dreamed and died. The generals are not the only ones remembered, or to remember.

Gettysburg—the Hallowed Ground

It was the bloodiest battle of the war. After his victory at Chancellorsville, Lee invaded Pennsylvania, determined to destroy the Union Army of the Potomac on its own soil. The fighting began on the morning of July 1,

Of the more than 2,000 monuments, markers and memorial tablets on the Gettysburg battlefield, the Pennsylvania Memorial is the largest.

1863 and was to last for three days. Under terrible strain and sacrifice by both sides, the Army of Northern Virginia, 70,000 strong, contested a larger force of 93,000 Union troops. On the evening of July 4 the Confederates retreated, ending Lee's last major offensive. The number of casualties totalled 51,000, a reflection of the high price of war. Then, four months later, a portion of the battlefield was dedicated as a burial ground. President Lincoln was not the major speaker, yet in 272 words he delivered a eulogy to be known forever as the "Gettysburg Address."

Gettysburg National Military Park and Gettysburg National Cemetery cover 25 square miles. You will find 31 miles of marked roads, with numerous monuments, memorials and statues along the way. Many of the states have erected monuments to their heroes. These include the imposing Virginia Memorial, surmounted by a statue of General Lee on his horse, Traveller; the North Carolina Memorial, designed by Gutzon Borglum (sculptor of the faces on Mt. Rushmore), located at the site where Lee rallied thousands of North Carolinians for the supreme effort on July 3; the

Hallowed Grounds

The first southern state memorial erected at Gettysburg honors the fighting men of Virginia as well as their confederate general, Robert E. Lee.

equestrian statue of General George C. Meade, on Cemetery Ridge; the Pennsylvania Monument, with statues of officers and the names of 35,000 men who fought in the ranks; and the Eternal Light Peace Memorial, dedicated by Franklin D. Roosevelt in 1938 (on the 75th anniversary of the battle) to "peace eternal in a nation united."

Get oriented at the National Park visitor center before you begin. Ask a lot of questions. Take time for the Electric Map orientation program. If you plan to visit Dwight Eisenhower's retirement farm at nearby Eisenhower National Historic Site, the Eisenhower Tour Information Center in the visitor center is the place to obtain tour tickets and to board the shuttle bus. By all means, take in the Cyclorama Center, adjacent to the visitor center, to see the 10-minute film; the circular Cyclorama, a mammoth painting depicting Pickett's Charge—a form of visual reporting of another day; and Lincoln's original Gettysburg Address (carefully sealed for environmental control) on display April through August.

At various locations along the auto tour route and elsewhere park rangers present programs and lead walks to interpret key events. Take advantage

A small detail of the third day's fighting from the Cyclorama painting, Gettysburg National Military Park.

of these activities; to get the true sense of place, the walking is at least as important as the driving.

Your first major stop after the visitor center should be at the High Water Mark, the setting of the climactic attack of the third day. The battle lines had been drawn in two sweeping arcs, with the Confederates on Seminary Ridge and the Union forces only a mile to the east on Cemetery Ridge. On July 3, after a heavy two-hour artillery barrage, a Confederate force of almost 12,000 under James Longstreet marched across open fields to attack the Federal center. Though they reached what has been called "the high water mark of the Confederacy," deadly Union fire shattered their ranks. Longstreet's men were forced to retreat with staggering losses. Lee's last major offensive was finished.

Take note of various trails you can follow on the battlefield. The High Water Mark Trail, 1/2-mile long, starts from the Cyclorama Center and leads past regimental monuments and a portion of an artillery battery to terrain defended by Union soldiers and the field headquarters of General Meade. (Trail guides are available at the Cyclorama Center.) The Big Round Top Loop, starting just beyond Auto Tour Stop 3, passes stone breastworks used during the battle, in a natural setting. Or walk to the group of boulders called Devil's Den, where Union troops were cleared in Longstreet's attack of July 2.

Allow time to join an interpretive walk at the national cemetery, a monumental setting yet something more. The Soldiers' National Monument is located near the spot where Lincoln spoke on November 19, 1863. The principal address, delivered by Edward Everett, might now be well forgotten, except as the prelude to Lincoln's remarks. Lincoln spoke briefly and simply, to his own time and to all time, expressing sorrow for the dead, and inspiration and challenge for the living.

Keep a sharp eye for turkey vultures and black vultures overhead; according to legend, such birds first appeared in the Gettysburg area in July 1863.

Travel tips and tidbits

There are several ways of touring the battlefield. The self-guiding auto tour is outlined in a park folder. If you prefer, for a set fee you can hire a licensed guide for a two-hour tour in your car, starting from the visitor center. Bus tours, tape tours and bicycles for rent are available nearby. All park roads are open to bicycling; tours outlined on park maps indicate recommended less-traveled roads. An eight-mile bridle trail begins at McMillan Woods and passes through battle areas of the second and third days of fighting.

Gettysburg in summer can be a very busy place. Because it is most crowded in midday hours and then hot in the afternoon, it's wise to join programs scheduled for early morning, late afternoon or evening. Make arrangements as early as possible to visit the Eisenhower National Historic Site or to engage a battlefield guide.

You'll find many commercial tourist attractions in the Gettysburg area. Follow your own preference, but choose carefully. Gettysburg College and Lutheran Theological Seminary are both of interest, having been used as Civil War hospitals; Dwight D. Eisenhower, in retirement following his presidency, maintained an office at Gettysburg College. The Gettysburg Travel Council Office and Information Center will furnish information about accommodations.

Events in Gettysburg include Apple Blossom Weekend, at South Mountain Fairgrounds, first weekend in May; Civil War Heritage Week, in late June and early July; Apple Harvest Festival, arts and crafts demonstrations at the Fairgrounds, guided tours of the area, first and second weekends in October; and the anniversary of Lincoln's Gettysburg Address, at the National Cemetery, November 19.

Maryland—Bloody Fighting in the Border State

Had it not been for immediate occupation by Federal troops, Maryland might have seceded and joined the Confederacy. Nonetheless, the state did become the setting of the bloodiest single day of the Civil War, when the Battle of Antietam (sometimes called the Battle of Sharpsburg) was fought on September 17, 1862. It was a major engagement with serious consequences, including an end to Lee's first campaign across the Potomac.

After a series of decisive victories, Lee had pressed to invade northern soil. He led a force of 41,000 against a much larger Union army of 87,000

"Peace Eternal in a Nation United" is one of the highlights on the self-guiding tour road at Gettysburg.

under McClellan. In addition to sheer numbers, the Union gained an added advantage when Indiana soldiers accidentally found Lee's orders wrapped around some cigars in Frederick, MD; thus, McClellan knew that Lee was splitting his forces, sending Stonewall Jackson to capture Harpers Ferry.

The fighting was fierce. More than 23,000 of both sides were killed or wounded before the day was done; at Sunken Road, henceforth to be known as Bloody Lane, 4,000 men fell in three hours. The Confederates withdrew across the Potomac on the night of September 18.

Though neither side gained a decisive victory, the battle was critical because British aid to the confederacy depended on its outcome. The indecisive McClellan delayed his pursuit, leading Lincoln to relieve him of command of the Army of the Potomac. Nevertheless, the Union's strategic victory gave Lincoln the basis for issuing the Emancipation Proclamation.

The visitor center, one mile north of Sharpsburg, features displays and an audiovisual orientation. Pick up a copy of the leaflet outlining the self-guiding auto tour. (You can also rent a taped narrative for use in your car.) Along eight miles of paved roads you'll see more than 200 iron tablets, monuments and battlefield maps. Note especially the vertical cannon barrels where six generals, three on each side, lost their lives and where a young

Hallowed Grounds

"Bloody Lane" as seen in a 1955 view of the Sunken Road, Antietam Battlefield. "The farmlands . . . should be left as they were . . . ."—House Committee on Military Affairs, 1902.

This colossal monument, "The Common Soldier," honors Civil Dead in Antietam National Cemetery.

Ohio commissary sergeant, William McKinley, later to be president of the United States, served hot coffee and food to his comrades.

When you visit Antietam National Cemetery, containing more than 5,000 graves, be sure to see the colossal granite monument to the Civil War dead, called "The Common Soldier," a powerful tribute to sacrifice and bravery.

Nearby Monocacy National Battlefield (three miles south of Frederick) preserves a site significant in later action. In July 1864, General Jubal Early brushed aside outer defenses to advance on Washington with a Confederate force of 23,000. On July 9, Union General Lew Wallace with 5,000 men slowed Early down in the bloody battle of Monocacy River. They didn't stop Early, yet saved the capital by gaining time. When rugged veterans were rushed north from southern Virginia, Washington, DC, was secure.

Monocacy is not a developed park, but it's interesting and scenic, an attractive spot off the beaten path for a walk in history. Bring a picnic lunch.

Travel tips and tidbits

Frederick, MD, was a focal point of operations for both sides during the war. At one time or another, cavalry skirmished in the streets. Barbara Fritchie, a legendary lady, reportedly gave a piece of her mind to Stonewall Jackson about his "rebel hordes." During the Battle of Antietam, thousands of wounded men were cared for here. In July 1864, the town was forced to pay $200,000 in ransom to Confederate General Jubal Early before he fought the Battle of Monocacy.

Frederick has many points of historic interest, including the reconstructed Barbara Fritchie House and the home of Roger Brooke Taney, the powerful chief justice of the Supreme Court who issued the Dred Scott decision. Francis Scott Key was born here and is buried at Mt. Olivet Cemetery, where the American flag flies over his grave day and night.

Civil War enthusiasts should consider a side trip to Harpers Ferry National Historical Park, close at hand in West Virginia. Not only was it the scene of John Brown's abolitionist raid in 1859, but once the war broke out Harpers Ferry became a strategic objective of the Confederacy. Before the Battle of Antietam, Stonewall Jackson captured 12,693 Union prisoners at Harpers Ferry, a town that changed hands many times during the war. Landmarks include John Brown's Fort and earthworks and gun emplacements used by Union and Confederate troops.

Clara Barton attended the wounded at a field hospital on the Antietam Battlefield (and did the same at Fredericksburg as well). Reminders of her life and times are displayed at Clara Barton National Historic Site at Glen Echo, MD, a surburb of Washington, DC. She founded the American Red Cross in 1881 and built this large house to be its headquarters.

Attractive Maryland state parks lie within reach of Antietam and Monocacy battlefields. Washington Monument State Park, three miles from Boonsboro, contains a museum with Civil War firearms and mementoes and an early stone monument to honor George Washington. Gathland State Park, just outside Burkittsville and once owned by George Townsend, a Civil War journalist, honors correspondents who covered the war. Gambrill State Park, five miles from Frederick, offers tent and trailer camping, and overlooks with expansive views of the historic countryside.

The Frederick Craft Fair, the first weekend in June, combines craft demonstrations, music and food. The Brunswick-Potomac River Festival, the first weekend in October, rekindles 19th century life on the C&O Canal with crafts, films and music.

Manassas—Two Major Battles

The Battle of First Manassas was the first major land battle of the war, fought on July 21, 1861 between raw volunteer troops of both sides for control of a key railroad junction. The following summer, the Battle of

Hallowed Grounds

Faced with a desperate situation in the Battle of Second Manassas, General Lee gambled boldly and forced the withdrawal of Union troops over the Stone Bridge.

Second Manassas (or Bull Run, as it was called in the North), pitted 73,000 Union troops against 55,000 Confederates. These engagements brought the reality of war to the backdoor of Washington, DC, and the starkness of its toll—24,000 men killed or wounded at Manassas alone.

The visitor center on Henry Hill should be your first stop. It's the most prominent site in the park, opening views of much of the battlefield. In the same building, the battlefield museum includes a three-dimensional electric map that will help you to understand the flow of action in both battles. Outside the museum the bold equestrian statue of General Thomas J. Jackson commemorates his arrival at the crucial hour of the first battle. Another officer, striving to rally his disorganized men, pointed to Jackson's line and shouted: "There stands Jackson like a stone wall! Rally behind the Virginians!" Thus, Jackson was given his immortal nickname. And before the day was done the desperate Confederate defense changed into an attack, sending the Union army back to Washington in a rout.

The Second Battle of Manassas was fought 13 months later, August 28-30, 1862. In that engagement Robert E. Lee outmaneuvered Union General John Pope for a decisive victory, leading to the Confederate invasion of Maryland, but the signs showed it would be a long and costly war. Take the driving tour to the key points in the 4,500-acre battlefield park, including the Stone Bridge, where Federal artillery opened the first battle; ruins of the Chinn House, used as a field hospital in both engagements and the scene of Longstreet's counterattack at Second Manassas; the Brawner Farm, where Jackson opened the Second Battle; and the Stone House, originally a tavern, but used as a field hospital in both battles.

Travel tips and tidbits

Consider a detour in your travels to New Market, VA, the site of one of the most spectacular events of the Civil War. It's a pleasant drive over the mountains and at New Market Battlefield Park your time will be well rewarded. Here, on May 15, 1864, cadets from Virginia Military Institute were pressed into action to hold a Confederate line, though 10 were killed and 47 wounded. The Hall of Valor commemorates their courage with exhibits and a film, while another movie traces Stonewall Jackson's Valley Campaign. New Market Battlefield Park is a private, non-profit area endowed by a VMI alumnus.

Prince William Forest Park, about midway between Manassas and Fredericksburg, provides choice camping. Administered by the National Park Service, Prince William Forest offers nature trails for hikers and bikers and backcountry fire roads for access to unspoiled areas.

Near the Manassas Visitor Center, General Thomas J. Jackson continues "Standing like a stonewall."

Fredericksburg—Between Two Capitals

Fredericksburg was destined to be engulfed, being midway between Washington and Richmond, on a good railroad, and with two strategically located rivers (the Rappahannock and Rapidan). It *was* engulfed, with intense fighting in and around the city, and changed hands seven times between 1861 and 1865. Now, more than a century later, miles of original trenches and gun pits remain; and along with narrative markers and monuments, they interpret the fields of action.

Hallowed Grounds

Wayside signs and markers and the carefully restored Old Salem Church help to relate only one of the many battles fought in and around Fredericksburg.

The Battle of Fredericksburg, December 13, 1862, was the first of four major engagements. It saw Union troops succeed in crossing the Rappahannock, to be driven back by Confederate fire. The following year, April 27 through May 6, 1863, the Confederates scored another victory at the Battle of Chancellorsville and Lee prepared for his second invasion of the North. But Stonewall Jackson was mortally wounded, by mistake, by his own men.

By 1864 the tide was turning. At the Battles of Wilderness, May 5-6, and Spotsylvania Court House, May 8-21, a determined Union army under Grant began the final drive that sealed the fate of the Confederacy. Neither battle produced a clear-cut victory, but strength and stamina were steadily sapped from the Confederates. Both sides suffered heavily in what has been called the most concentrated fighting ever seen on this continent.

The full tour route of Fredericksburg and Spotsylvania National Military Park is 70 miles long. To cover the four battlefields it is best to allow two full days, with about a half-day for each battlefield. Bring a good pair of walking shoes. Cassette tours are available at the Fredericksburg Visitor Center.

Start your tour at the Chancellorsville Visitor Center, where you'll learn how Lee outmaneuvered Union General Joseph Hooker, who was forced to withdraw across the Rappahannock. After Chancellorsville, go to the visitor center in Fredericksburg, then tour the battlefield in town. Be sure to take in Chatham Manor, a Georgian brick manor house, which Federal forces used as an artillery and communications center, then as a field hospital where Clara Barton and Walt Whitman nursed the wounded. The site of several pontoon bridges over which Union troops crossed the Rappahannock is nearby. You can also see where Longstreet's men fired point-blank from Marye's Heights and the Sunken Road at charging Federals, forcing them to retreat across the river.

Both sides suffered heavily in all the battles around Fredericksburg. More than 15,000 Union soldiers, including 12,000 unidentified, are buried at the National Cemetery here. One of the most poignant memorials in the park is the statue near the Fredericksburg Battlefield Visitor Center depicting a Confederate sergeant who left his lines to administer water to the wounded and dying of the Union army.

The most significant casualty, as mentioned above, was Stonewall Jackson. The house where he died is included in the park, yet separate from the battlefields, at Guinea, 15 miles south of Fredericksburg. Why so removed? After the accidental shooting, Jackson's arm was amputated at a field station. Fearing that Jackson might be captured, Lee directed that he be taken from Chancellorsville, 25 miles to "Fairfield" at Guinea Station. There his condition worsened and pneumonia set in. "Let us cross over the river, and rest under the shade of the trees," Jackson murmured just before he died.

During the Civil War, the Lacey House (now Chatham Manor) was used as headquarters for Union officers, then as a hospital in 1862.

101

Travel tips and tidbits

Enthusiasts of formal gardens will enjoy the restored Colonial Revival Garden at Chatham Manor, complete with columnar evergreens, arbors and covered walkways, parterres and geometric flower beds. In the 18th century, Chatham was the home of William Fitzhugh, one of Virginia's wealthiest landowners. It was restored as a beautiful estate in the early 20th century and donated to the National Park Service in 1975.

Avoid confusion between the Fredericksburg Battlefield Visitor Center, maintained by the National Park Service, and Fredericksburg Visitor Center, which is operated by the city at 706 Caroline Street to provide information on other historical attractions and accommodations in and near the city.

Picnic facilities are available at each battlefield unit as well as Chatham and Stonewall Jackson Memorial Shrine. There is no overnight camping in the park, but Prince William Forest Park, 23 miles north, has very good camping sites, and there are private campgrounds in the area.

For hikers/walkers an excellent seven-mile loop trail connects important sites in the Spotsylvania Court House section of the park. Pick up a brochure before starting. Other interpretive trails are located along the Sunken Road, at Old Salem Church, and between Hazel Grove and Fairview at Chancellorsville.

Special events in the park include the 11 a.m. Memorial Day ceremony in the National Cemetery and the annual program commemorating the Battle of Fredericksbrug, held at the Richard Kirkland Monument the nearest Sunday to December 14.

You may want to take a side trip to George Washington Birthplace National Monument, 38 miles east of Fredericksburg (treated in detail in Tour V). Fredericksburg itself has many points of interest associated with the Washington family.

Richmond and Petersburg—Nearing the End

For four long, hard years, from the very beginning of the Civil War, "On to Richmond" was the rallying cry of Union troops. Richmond, VA, was the capital of the Confederacy, its principal manufacturing and medical center, and its primary supply depot for the Eastern theater of war. Little wonder that seven military drives were directed at Richmond. Of them all, two—McClellan's Peninsula campaign of 1862 and Grant's assault of 1864—brought Union troops within sight of the capitol. But they advanced no closer. It took Grant's devastating siege of Petersburg to force the Confederates to abandon Richmond.

Richmond National Battlefield Park, VA, today contains 10 park units. Located in a loop east and south of the city, they offer a many-sided insight to the tragic war period. A complete tour of the park involves a 100-mile

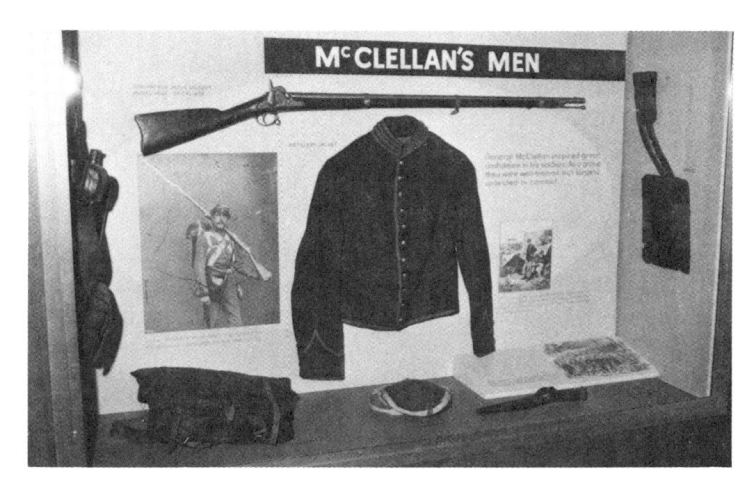

Exhibits in the Chimborazo and Fort Harrison visitor centers display objects from Richmond battlefields.

Richmond National Battlefield Park is one of many Civil War sites where demonstrations are a part of the interpretive program.

drive, which begins at Chimborazo Visitor Center, once the site of a major Confederate military hospital. Exhibits, battlefield tour maps and the audiovisual program will orient you.

Drive north on the tour route to visit such points as Chickahominy Bluff, a part of the outer Confederate line defending Richmond, where Lee watched the beginning of the Seven Days' Battles of 1862; Gaines' Mill, where you can still see shallow trenches defended by Union soldiers; and Cold Harbor, where Grant's army suffered 7,000 casualties in less than 30 minutes.

Hallowed Grounds

The tour route south leads to the Fort Harrison vicinity, the scene of dramatic action after Grant crossed the James River to direct his main effort against Petersburg. In a surprise attack on September 29, 1864, Union soldiers captured Fort Harrison, forcing realignment of Richmond's southern defenses. The Fort Harrison Visitor Center provides interpretive displays on the battle, including the gallantry of black troops, 14 of whom were awarded the Congressional Medal of Honor.

Due south of Richmond, Petersburg was the scene of Lee's final struggle against Grant. The 10 months of grim siege warfare began in the summer of 1864, with Grant's huge army continually hammering at Lee's veterans, stubbornly protecting their capital and the Petersburg rail center.

A one-way, four-mile auto tour, starting from the visitor center, leads to many well defined points of interest at Petersburg National Battlefield. From Battery 5, Grant shelled Petersburg with "The Dictator," a 17,000-pound seacoast mortar. At Battery 9, a trail leads to Meade's Station, which President Lincoln visited during the fighting, near Fort Stedman, the site of "Lee's Last Great Offensive." The Maine Monument memorializes the greatest regimental loss of the war.

The most engrossing part of the battlefield surrounds the section called the Crater. Here Union troops from Pennsylvania, who had been coal

A "living history" camp, alongside the Petersburg Tour Road, where historians provide descriptions and demonstrations of the Petersburg siege.

104

miners, dug a tunnel under a Confederate fort and exploded four tons of gunpowder. The explosion killed 278 men, destroyed an artillery battery, and created an immense crater. In the fighting that followed, the Confederates recaptured the site, while the Union lost 4,000 men—killed, wounded or captured.

During the long siege, the two armies were in almost constant contact. The Confederate lines stretched farther and farther as they tried to block the Union's attempts to surround the city. Lee ultimately evacuated Petersburg and Richmond on April 2, 1865 and turned to the west.

One of the most impressive parts of the park is located away from the battlefield. At City Point, bordering the James and Appomatox Rivers in the historic community of Hopewell, General Grant maintained his headquarters. It was plainly a very busy place, a center of communications and of supplies to sustain the siege. Grant's cabin was one of 23 structures built in the headquarters complex for use by his staff officers. President Lincoln visited Grant twice at City Point, which served as command headquarters until March 29, 1865, when Grant moved close to the action.

City Point has not been drastically altered since those days. When he chose the site, Grant's headquarters tents occupied the front lawn of an imposing mansion which the Eppes family had started before the American Revolution. That building still stands, with several rooms containing Eppes furnishings, open to the public.

You can also see Grant's two-room log cabin on its original site. After the war it was disassembled and taken to Philadelphia as a memorial to General Grant. However, with the acquisition of City Point by the National Park

Of the thousands of cabins built by the Army during the Civil War,, General U.S. Grant's cabin at City Point is the only one known to have survived.

105

Hallowed Grounds

Service in 1979, the cabin was returned to its original location here. It is exactly the type of facility—simple and straightforward—to expect of the earthy Ulysses S. Grant.

Travel tips and tidbits

Richmond is rich in Civil War sites, including the Virginia capitol, designed by Thomas Jefferson, which served as capitol of the Confederacy; the White House of the Confederacy, home of Jefferson Davis from 1861 to 1865, now the centerpiece of the Museum of the Confederacy; the Lee House, the home rented to Robert E. Lee during the war (presently closed to the public); and Hollywood Cemetery, burial place of U.S. presidents James Monroe and John Tyler, Confederate president Jefferson Davis, General J.E.B. Stuart, and 18,000 Confederate soldiers.

Ten of Richmond's principal points of interest are linked on a self-guiding walking tour starting from the State capitol. Pick up a walking tour brochure at one of the Richmond Visitor Centers (at Exit 14 off I-95/64 or downtown in the 6th Street Market Place and Main Street Station). Travel counselors at these centers will help with accommodations. For statewide information, stop at the Commonwealth of Virginia's vacation information center, a few steps from the capitol.

One of the most interesting drives (or walks) in Richmond covers 1.3 miles of Monument Avenue, lined with trees and restored homes. Statues on the avenue include those of Robert E. Lee, Stonewall Jackson and Jefferson Davis. The Maggie L. Walker National Historic Site,

During the summer at Petersburg National Battlefield, a Confederate artillery crew demonstrates the live firing of their six-horse-drawn field piece.

in Jackson Ward, preserves the restored home of the daughter of an ex-slave, who rose to prominence in business and public service. It is treated in detail in Tour V.

While touring the City Point unit of Petersburg National Battlefield, allow time for a walk in the adjacent City Point Historic District. It commemorates one of the nation's oldest communities, settled in 1613. The Historic District was established by the Hopewell City Council in 1979, complementing the feeling and flavor of the national park unit. Appomattox Manor actually remained in the Eppes family from 1635 until December 1979, when the house and 13 acres were acquired by the Federal government and transferred to the National Park Service.

Petersburg's Old Blandford Church, built in 1735, a field hospital during the Civil War, was restored in 1901 as a Confederate shrine featuring 15 stained glass windows designed by Louis Tiffany. Centre Hill Mansion, a restored mansion of the Federal period, is furnished with elaborate local antiques. Sunday concerts are given during fall, winter and spring.

Appomattox Court House National Historical Park is famous as the site of General Lee's surrender to General Grant in 1865.

Appomattox Court House—Where Lee and Grant Meet

One week earlier, Lee had left Petersburg, heading west, hoping to join with Confederate forces still fighting in North Carolina. After a final attack on April 9, it became clear that further resistance was futile. Lee elected to surrender.

In the parlor of Wilmer McLean's home at Appomattox Court House, General U.S. Grant triumphed . . . "without exultation, and with a noble respect of his enemy." Here, the four-year-old Civil War came to a close.

Appomattox Court House, where Grant and Lee met on April 9, 1865, was a county seat and a stop on the stage road between Richmond (100 miles east) and Lynchburg (20 miles west). It was an active rural community of homes, stores and offices. The setting, even now, is still rural. Appomattox Court House has somehow survived progress to remain a quiet, uncrowded and relatively uncommercialized cameo of history.

Though definitely off the well-worn tourist paths, Appomattox Court House is a joy to visit. Allow enough time, at least half a day, to take in (leisurely) all of the park and to hear the interpretive talks given at various points. Appomattox Court House National Historical Park is small enough to see it all on foot (with a good pair of walking shoes).

The appearance of the village faithfully represents the day the Civil War came to a close. Some structures standing then are now gone, victims of time and neglect, but 13 of the original buildings of April 1865 still remain, while nine others have been reconstructed on their own sites.

The place to begin, in fact, is the reconstructed courthouse building, now the visitor center of the park. Though the interior is greatly altered, the exterior is faithful to the appearance of the original. Exhibits and audiovisual programs relate the historic events.

After getting your bearings, walk the village lanes. The courthouse actually played no role in the surrender, for it was closed that day, Palm Sunday. Thus, the meeting between Grant and Lee took place at the three-

Along a muddy road, in front of the widow Kelly's house, the Confederate arms were stacked for the last time.

story brick McLean House. Lee arrived first. Then Grant came, entering the parlor where Lee was waiting. According to a dispatch in the New York Herald, the meeting at the outset was very nearly a private one. After some conversation, General Grant's staff officers were called in and formally presented. The dialogue was sober, confined mostly to business.

A spirit of mutual respect prevailed. Grant's terms allowed Confederate officers to keep their side arms and soldiers to keep their horses and mules to work their farms. "It will be very gratifying and do much toward conciliating our people," responded Lee. Three days later, Confederate troops marched before the Union Army, laid down their flags, stacked their weapons, and headed home at last.

The sturdy brick Clover Hill Tavern is another key point of interest. Built in 1819 (which makes it the oldest structure in the village), it served travelers and stage lines on the Richmond-Lynchburg Stage Road. In the two downstairs rooms of the restored tavern you can see where many of the paroles were printed for the surrendered Confederates. The other room contains exhibits dealing with the paroling process.

The store, law office, widow Kelly's house and slave quarters also tell of life in rural "southside" Virginia. Outside the village itself several other

Hallowed Grounds

The two-story, brick courthouse was destroyed by fire in 1892. It was reconstructed in 1963-64 and is used as the park's visitor center.

sites are well worth visiting, including Lee's headquarters where he pondered the decision to surrender, and Grant's headquarters on the night of April 9, 1865. Ask for directions at the visitor center.

Travel tips and tidbits

As a side trip, consider following the route Lee took in his retreat from Petersburg to Appomattox. Most of the roads still exist today and the countryside has not been radically altered. Starting from the visitor center at Petersburg Battlefield, the distance to Appomattox Court House is 112 miles, but the combination of narrow back roads and stops for State historical markers will make it a trip of four to five hours. Points to note enroute include Amelia, Jetersville, and Farmville. Sayler's Creek Battlefield Historical State Park (where the Union advance caught up with the rear of Lee's army and captured 6,000 men) features an interpretive auto route. Two excellent interpretive guides to this route written by Chris Caulkins, a National Park Service historian, are available for purchase at park book shops.

Check at the Appomattox Visitor Center for extra events above and beyond the usual interpretive activities. Though Appomattox Court House National Historical Park does not have a specific calendar of events, various Civil War re-enactment groups are likely to hold authentic encampments on summer weekends with demonstrations and explanations for the public.

Basic camping facilities are located nearby at Holiday Lake State Park, nine miles northeast of Appomattox. Lynchburg, 24 miles west, is well supplied with motels and eating establishments. It's an easy drive north to Charlottesville or west to the Blue Ridge Parkway (about 1½ hours for each) and not much farther to Lexington, where Robert E. Lee served as president of Washington and Lee College (now University) following the Civil War, and is buried.

Hallowed Grounds

Park Information

Antietam National Battlefield
P.O. Box 158
Sharpsburg, MD 21782
(301) 432-5124

Visitor Center—From Pennsylvania Turnpike (Gettysburg Pike Exit) to 15S to 70W toward Hagerstown and Route 65S. From Washington, D.C. take 270W to Frederick—take 70W Hagerstown and route 65S.

Visitor Center hours 8:30—5:00 winter; 8:00—6:00 from mid-May to August.

Appomattox Court House National Historical Park
R.O. Box 218, Rt. 24
Appomattox, VA 24522
(804) 352-8987

Visitor Center—Two miles north of the Town of Appomattox, VA, and follow signs to park visitor center (restored courthouse building).

Visitor Center hours 9:00—5:00

Fredericksburg and Spotsylvania National Military Park
P.O. Box 679
Fredericksburg, VA 22404
(703) 373-4461

Visitor Center—The visitor center is at 1013 Lafayette Boulevard in the city of Fredericksburg, which is at the intersection of Lafayette Boulevard with historic Sunken Road. Lafayette Boulevard is Business Route 1 (U.S.). The visitor center is in the southwestern corner of the city.

Visitor Center hours—Fredericksburg Battlefield Visitor Center 9:00—5:00 daily, year round; 8:30—6:30 in summer; 9:00—6:00 on spring and fall weekends.

Chancellorsville Visitor Center: 9:00—5:00 daily year round; 8:30—6:30 during summer.

Chancellorsville Visitor Center—located on U.S. Route 3, about ten miles west of Fredericksburg, and seven miles west of Route I-95.

Chancellorsville Visitor Center is the most completely acessible of the park's buildings to handicapped visitors.

Gettysburg National Military Park
Taneytown Road
Gettysburg, PA 17325
(717) 334-1124

Visitor Center—One mile south of Gettysburg town square on Business Route 15. From Washington (the south), take business 15 (Steinwehr Avenue exit) off 15. Visitor Center will be on right as you enter town. From east, west, or north, go to town square and take Baltimore Street south. At second light, bear right. Visitor Center will be on left two blocks ahead.

Visitor Center hours 8:00—5:00 daily. Closed Christmas, New Years, and Thanksgiving Days.

Manassas National Battlefield Park
Box 1830
Manassas, VA 22110
(703) 754-7107

Visitor Center—From I-66 take Manassas exit. On Rt. 234 north of Manassas I-66 exit.

Visitor Center hours 8:30—6:00 summer; 9:00—5:00 winter.

Petersburg National Battlefield
P.O. Box 549, Off Highway 36
Petersburg, VA 23804
(804) 732-3531

Visitor Center—Entrance to the main unit is off of VA Highway 36, 2 miles east of downtown Petersburg, VA. Visitor Center is at the beginning of the park tour road, a 4-mile, one way drive. Other units are also open to the public.

Visitor Center hours 8:00—5:00 (winter); 8:00—7:00 (summer).

Richmond National Battlefield Park
3215 E. Broad Street
Richmond, VA 23223
(804) 226-1986

Visitor Center—Chimborazo Visitor Center—east of downtown area at 3215 E. Broad Street.

Visitor Center hours—Chimborazo Visitor Center 9:00—5:00

Visitor Center—Fort Harrison—Battlefield Park Road off Route 5, east of Richmond.

Visitor Center hours—Ft. Harrison Visitor Center 9:30—5:30.

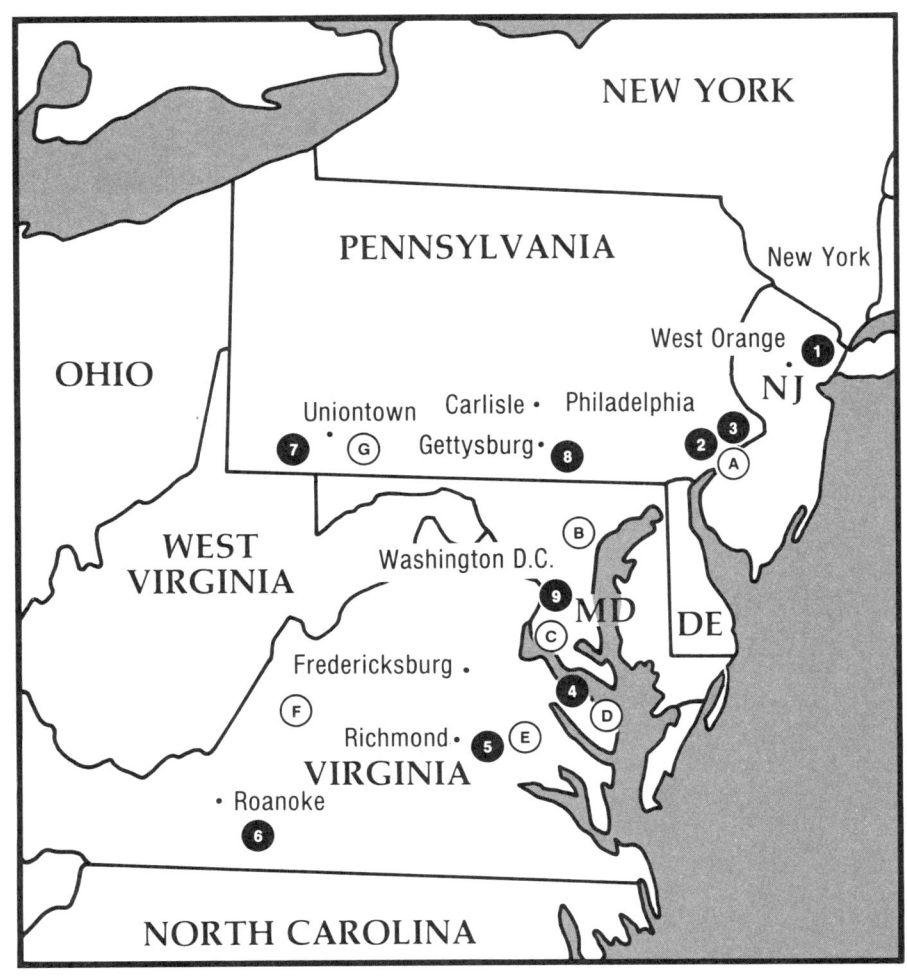

Tour Five
1. Edison National Historic Site
2. Independence National Historic Park
3. Edgar Allan Poe National Historic Site
4. George Washington Birthplace National Monument
5. Maggie L. Walker National Historic Site
6. Booker T. Washington National Monument
7. Friendship Hill National Historic Site
8. Eisenhower National Historic Site
9. Clara Barton National Historic Site

Additional Sights
(A) Bartram's Garden
(B) Ft. McHenry National Monument
(C) Mount Vernon
(D) Stratford Hall
(E) Richmond National Battlefield Park
(F) Blue Ridge Parkway and Shenandoah National Park
(G) Ft. Necessity National Battlefield

Tour Five

Of Men and Women Who Inspired the Nation
A Great Americans Tour

National parks memorialize struggles and achievements of people of all kinds—the daring, determined, those of genius, and those who served. They are native Americans who greeted the first "settlers" from Europe; they are immigrants from around the world, and their descendants. They are men and women, presidents and poets, educators and business people—pioneers in diverse fields.

The lives and careers of all the personalities whose homes, or other specially related sites, are treated on this tour spark inspiration. They were leaders, each in his or her own way. George Washington appears to have been endowed with modesty, humility, and deep concern for his fellows, regardless of their station. Booker T. Washington's life serves as an example of dedication and humanitarian service in the struggle for full citizenship for his people, against overwhelming obstacles.

Starting in the northern part of New Jersey, the first park on this tour, Edison National Historic Site, interprets the life of Thomas A. Edison, the great inventor, who rose from hunble beginnings and was motivated by an intense drive to learn and create. From north Jersey it's an easy drive to

Philadelphia to pursue the fascinating life and times of Benjamin Franklin. He called himself simply "Benjamin Franklin, Printer," but he was Philadelphia's uncommon citizen as you can readily see at Independence National Historical Park and elsewhere in the city. Also in Philadelphia, a visit to the Edgar Allan Poe National Historic Site reveals Poe's pioneering contributions to literature as well as his own particular lifestyle.

Continuing south from Philadelphia, the setting of George Washington Birthplace National Monument, in the "Northern Neck" of Virginia, is like a living vestige of the 18th century, a worthy memorial to the father of this country. It is located 50 miles south of Mount Vernon on the Potomac River in Westmoreland County, Virginia. From the Washington family's colonial plantation it's only a short drive to Richmond, where the Maggie L. Walker National Historic Site memorializes a prominent black American, who was born the daughter of a slave. Guests at Mrs. Walker's red brick home over the years included distinguished black contemporaries, such as W.E.B. Dubois, Booker T. Washington and Mary McLeod Bethune.

Also in Virginia, Booker T. Washington National Monument tells not only the story of a man born in slavery who rose to eminence, but also something of what may be found in all great Americans. "The individual who can do something that the world wants done," he wrote, "will, in the end, make his way regardless of race."

If you are coming from the west, your first stop should be Friendship Hill National Historic Site, midway between Uniontown, PA, and Morgantown, WV. The home of Albert Gallatin, a statesman of extraordinary talent, unfolds a romantic and adventurous story of immigration from the Old World to the New. This leads logically to Gettysburg, the site of the only home ever owned by Dwight D. Eisenhower and his wife, where they lived at times when he was President and after he retired. It is 50 miles south of where his ancestors had settled in the 18th century. Eisenhower National Historic Site shows the lifestyle of this great American after he found "an escape from concrete into the countryside."

Thomas Edison at Work and at Home

At West Orange, NJ, the Edison Laboratory, which the great inventor built in 1887 and made his headquarters for 44 years, looks much as he left it. Here, at Edison National Historic Site, you can learn about his inventions and the "invention factory"—which we now call the "research and development laboratory"—that he pioneered.

Thomas A. Edison, known as "The Wizard of Menlo Park," at work in his "invention factory," which he build in 1887 at West Orange, NJ.

On December 6, 1877, in what is now the Menlo Park section of Edison Township, the 30-year-old wizard invented the phonograph. Two years later he perfected the first practical incandescent light and in 1880 built the first electric railway locomotive (which ran 1½ miles). He also invented the mimeograph, motion picture camera, telephone transmitter and other instruments that characterize the 20th century. Join a guided tour to view his chemistry lab, machine shop, library (including the cot on which he took cat naps between long hours of work), and the "Black Maria," a reconstruction of Edison's motion picture studio—the world's first. You'll also see

Glenmont, Edison's victorian home, is included in Edison National Historic Site.

that classic vintage film, "The Great Train Robbery," and hear original Edison recordings played on early phonographs. Note that Edison experimented with a variety of plants; he was extremely interested in the uses of wild flora for many purposes.

The park includes Edison's home, a spacious Victorian mansion called "Glenmont," located one-half mile from the Laboratory, in a private subdivision. The house is furnished much as it was when he lived in it, with heirlooms and family portraits and the desk he called his "thought bench." The home would be fascinating in its own right, but it's especially so because of the Edison association. Contact the park staff at the laboratory for tour information and hours.

Travel tips and tidbits

While driving south from West Orange, stop to see the Edison Memorial Tower, a few miles from New Brunswick, NJ, at exit 131 off the Garden State Parkway. This 131-foot tower, topped by a 14-foot high electric light bulb, stands on the spot where Edison made the first incandescent light bulb in 1879.

For your travels elsewhere: The Henry Ford Museum and Greenfield Village, at Dearborn, MI, conceived by Henry Ford as a tribute to American culture and resourcefulness, were dedicated in 1929 to Thomas Edison. The Menlo Park laboratory is among the historic buildings which were moved to Dearborn from many parts of the country. At Fort Myers, FL, the Thomas Edison Botanical Gardens and Laboratory show where the wizard of electricity maintained his winter home amid 14 acres of rare trees, ferns and flowers.

As an author, printer and publisher, scientist and inventor, statesman and diplomat, Benjamin Franklin did so many things so well.

Franklin—A Man for All Times

For all his renown, Benjamin Franklin appears to have been proudest of his printing trade. As a boy in Boston, with merely two years of formal schooling and one of 15 children born to a humble family, Franklin worked as an apprentice printer before reaching his teens. By the time he was 17 he was ready to leave Boston. He fled to the rising commercial metropolis of Philadelphia, where he emerged as an American of rare accomplishments.

Pursue the fascinating life of Franklin in his chosen city by starting at Franklin Court, on the south side of Market Street between Third and Fourth Streets. Though the house in which he lived is long gone, it is by no means forgotten. Following extensive archaeological digging, the National Park Service decided not to try a reconstruction, but rather to undertake a major interpretation worthy of Franklin.

Of Men and Women Who Inspired the Nation

The site is outlined by a large steel frame known as a ghost structure. The entire Franklin Court complex, along with trees and gardens, was given one of America's foremost architectural awards by President Ronald Reagan. The courtyard has been re-created to reflect the scene of an earlier day. A ramp leads to a large underground museum that would intrigue "Old Ben" himself. In one exhibit the visitor can pick up a tele-

Ben Franklin's home in Philadelphia was located behind row houses facing Market Street. Modern steel "ghost" structures outline his home and print shop in Franklin Court.

phone and dial famous Americans and Europeans to hear their views of this most remarkable man—the printer, publisher, philosopher, patriot, statesman, inventor, and human being whose long life was marked both by happy and sad times.

Five bordering row houses on Market Street (three of which he owned) have been restored and adapted to interpret various phases of Franklin's career. The Print Shop (320 Market) depicts 18th century printing (with actual demonstrations) and its social and political influences. The post office (316 Market) commemorates Franklin's role as first postmaster of the United States. Mail your letters here with the famous hand-stamped postmark, "B. Free Franklin."

Franklin Court is only one of several sites in Independence National Historical Park closely associated with Franklin. At Independence Hall, he was the oldest member of the Continental Congress, and signer of both the Declaration of Independence and the Constitution. Philosophical Hall, home of the American Philosophical Society, traces its origin to Franklin; so does Library Hall, a reconstruction of the original building of the Library company founded by Franklin in 1731. Christ Church, a building of classic 18th century architecture, was attended by both Washington and Franklin; at Christ Church cemetery (Fifth and Arch Streets) an unpretentious stone slab, simply inscribed, marks the burial place of Benjamin Franklin and his wife, Deborah.

Travel tips and tidbits

Benjamin Franklin's influence is manifest in various parts of Philadelphia. The Benjamin Franklin Institute, at 20th and Benjamin Franklin Parkway, has been a leader in scientific progress since its founding in 1824. Original artifacts associated with Franklin's life and work are among its abundant displays. James Earle Fraser's massive marble statue of Franklin, in the main Institute building, was designated by Congress in 1972 as the Benjamin Franklin National Memorial.

The Franklin tree, or **Franklinia alatamaha**, *celebrated in the world of horticulture, grows at Bartram's Garden, 54th Street and Lindberg Boulevard, on the shore of the Schuylkill River. Franklin knew this place well, coming to visit his friend, John Bartram, the great natural botanist at that time. On a collecting tour in the wilds of Georgia, Bartram and his son, William, discovered and brought home to Philadelphia the* **Franklinia***, which has not been seen in the wild since 1802. Afternoon tea and tours of Bartram's Garden are offered Tuesday through Friday afternoons.*

Edgar Allan Poe was one of America's greatest poets, short-story writers and literary critics.

Edgar Allan Poe—Literary Pioneer

Edgar Allan Poe lived in many places, including Richmond, Boston, Baltimore, and New York. He studied for a year at the University of Virginia, and again at West Point, searching for his star in a life that lasted only 40 years—from 1809 to 1849. The six years he spent in Philadelphia were his most productive and, perhaps, his most content. For part of that time, until 1844, he lived in the small brick house which he mentioned as follows: "My address is 234 North Seventh Street above Spring Garden, west side." (Today the site's address is 532 North Seventh Street.)

A visit to Edgar Allan Poe National Historic Site—two buildings containing his home and exhibits—tells a great deal about the writer and his influence. Poe opened the doors to new approaches of writing mystery,

Poe's Spring Garden home today; enter 532 N. 7th Street, above Spring Garden.

adventure and terror; he pioneered in science fiction and the detective story. Of all American poems, Poe's "The Raven" may be the best known.

One can only wonder what great works he might have created had he been given a longer life. His Philadelphia years were indeed prolific: he produced such classics as "The Gold Bug" and "The Fall of the House of Usher," while at the same time serving as editor of popular literary magazines.

Of the several Philadelphia houses where Poe lived at one time or another, only this one survives, thanks to the efforts of the late Richard Gimbel, a devoted Poe scholar and collector. Congress in 1980 chose the site to memorialize Poe as an American pioneering spirit.

Travel tips and tidbits

You can visit several other sites associated with Edgar Allan Poe while traveling this tour route. The Edgar Allan Poe House and Museum, 203 N. Amity Street, preserves the Baltimore home he occupied from 1832 to 1835. His grave is also in Baltimore, at Westminster Presbyterian Church, Fayette and Greene Streets. While in Richmond, visit the Edgar Allan Poe Museum, 1914 East Main Street, in the Old Stone House, built in 1737 and believed to be Richmond's oldest surviving stone building. At Charlottesville, Poe as a student occupied Room 13, West Range, at the University of Virginia. And should you be in New York City at any time, visit the Edgar Allen Poe Cottage, in the Bronx, to see his last home.

Of Men and Women Who Inspired the Nation

This reconstructed memorial manor is representative of an 18th century plantation house commemorating George Washington's birth at Popes Creek Plantation.

The Washington Beginning

Many travelers are suprised to learn that George Washington was not born at Mount Vernon, the great mansion overlooking the Potomac River a few miles south of Washington, DC. Mount Vernon was his home only in adulthood and where he died in 1799. He was born at a lesser known site 38 miles east of Fredericksburg in the Northern Neck of Virginia. The pastoral feeling of Washington's time still prevails.

The plantation that overlooks Popes Creek and the Potomac already was an established family farm at the time of Washington's birth on February 22, 1732. The first of the family to arrive on the scene had been his great-grandfather, an officer aboard an English ship, *Seahorse of London*. It arrived in Virginia in 1657 for a cargo of tobacco and ran aground during a storm.

In those early days, great plantations flourished on the Northern Neck, a slender finger of land pointing into Chesapeake Bay. In 1858, the Commonwealth of Virginia took action to rescue this precious fragment of its past, acquiring a part of the land, which (in 1882) was donated to the Federal government. Through efforts of the Wakefield National Memorial Association, considerable restoration and recovery were achieved during the 1920's and 1930's. In 1932, the 200th anniversary of Washington's

George Washington Birthplace National Monument is a colonial working farm overlooking Popes Creek estuary and the Potomac River in Westmoreland County, Virginia.

birth, the national monument was officially opened—one of the first units of the National Park System in the East.

The two most prominent features are the memorial house and kitchen, now attended by guides in period costumes. The house, overlooking Popes Creek, was built in 1930-31 to represent a typical 18th century plantation home, with bricks handmade from the clay of an adjoining field. The interior includes a round tilt-top table, which tradition says was in the original house when it burned. The house contains many other furnishings of the 1730-50 period. The kitchen is also completely furnished with colonial equipment and utensils.

The living farm shows agricultural activities as they may have been conducted when Washington was a child. Livestock, poultry and crops are of old varieties, cultivated and harvested by colonial methods, with something special in every season. In spring, newborn animals make their debut into the world; apple, peach, and cherry trees blossom in the orchard; and the fields are plowed for new crops. Gardeners will especially appreciate the colonial herb and kitchen gardens, with 18th century flowers, herbs, fruits, and vegetables in formal plantings, all tagged with their common names. As well as being pleasing to the eye, these plants were used for scent, cooking and medicine.

There are many acres of natural beauty. The walking trail at the picnic area runs through woods and marshlands, providing the opportunity to view and photograph songbirds and wildflowers. From mid-October to mid-March, Popes Creek and the Potomac become a major attraction as the home of thousands of migratory waterfowl including whistling swans and Canada geese.

Walk or drive one mile north of the memorial house to the burying ground where Washington's father, grandfather and great-grandfather are buried. Here you can examine exact replicas of two of America's earliest burial stones, plus five memorial tablets erected in the 1930's. George and Martha Washington are buried at Mount Vernon.

Travel tips and tidbits

There is always something on the park's calendar of activities and events to make the visitor feel close to Washington and his time in history. ("A Childhood Place," a 14-minute film on life at Popes Creek, is shown regularly at the visitor center.) Activities include an Independence Day Celebration on July 4th; an annual Colonial Crafts Festival in mid-July; and regularly scheduled archaeology walks, garden tours, and music recitals. In seasons other than summer, there are demonstrations of plantation crafts such as woodworking, blacksmithing and leatherworking, spinning and weaving.

Nearby Fredericksburg is rich in Washington family connections. Kenmore, one of the finest restorations in Virginia, was the home of Washington's sister, Betty, and her husband, Colonel Fielding Lewis. The Mary Washington House was purchased by George for his mother, and she lived there until her death. The Rising Sun Tavern was built by Washington's youngest brother, Charles; it has been restored and refurnished with the accessories of "a proper tavern." The Fredericksburg Visitor Center, in the heart of the city's historic district, offers a 12-minute slide program on attractions and history, free visitor parking passes, and tour information.

Stratford Hall, seven miles east of the national monument, is the ancestral estate of the Lees of Virginia and birthplace of Robert E. Lee. The massive Great House, built about 1725, is considered one of the finest examples of early Georgian architecture in this country. The Stratford dining room serves a plantation lunch April through October. Westmoreland State Park, between Washington's Birthplace and Stratford Hall, offers camping, swimming, and hiking trails.

Maggie L. Walker was the daughter of a slave living in Richmond, VA. Born shortly after the Civil War, she became prominent in banking, social organizations and civil rights.

The Penny Banker at Home

On Leigh Street in the Jackson Ward Historic District of Richmond, VA, the Maggie L. Walker National Historic Site preserves the impressive redbrick home, complete with all its furnishings, as a memorial to Maggie L. Walker. She was a prominent black American, born shortly after the Civil War (in 1867) and lived a fruitful life until her death in 1934.

"What's important about Maggie Walker?" asked William Penn Mott, Director of the National Park Service, when he came to dedicate the site at ceremonies in 1985. It was a rhetorical question which he proceeded to answer:

"She was the daughter of a slave living in Richmond right after the Civil War. She developed a penny bank that went right through the depression without failing; developed an emporium; developed a school. What a tremendous personality she was.

The Maggie L. Walker National Historic Site is located in the famous 1920 Jackson Ward community of Richmond, VA.

"What does this mean? It means that people can go there, hear that story and be inspired: 'By golly, I can do it if she can do it!' That's as important as going to Yosemite."

Mrs. Walker was president of the Council of Colored Women, vice president of the Negro Organization Society of Virginia, and a board member of the National Association for the Advancement of Colored People. With Congressional action in 1978, the Maggie L. Walker National Historic Site was established; thus, the role of black Americans was recognized as one of Richmond's valuable assets. She was the friend of such black leaders as Booker T. Washington, W.E.B. DuBois, Marcus Garvey and Mary McLeod Bethune.

The two-story house stayed in her family until 1979 when it was acquired by the Federal government. A five-year restoration project returned it to its 1920's appearance, when the Jackson Ward community was a prosperous residential area adjacent to a thriving black financial and business community.

Travel tips and tidbits

Two blocks from the Maggie L. Walker home, the Bill "Bojangles" Robinson Statue, at the corner of Leigh and Adams Streets, honors the world's greatest tap dancer, "Mr. Bojangles." He was born in 1878 at 915 N. Third Street, starred in stage and film hits and died in 1949. The Virginia E. Randolph Museum, at 2200 Mountain Road, Glen Allen, is in the converted home of Virginia E. Randolph, an outstanding black educator and founder of vocational education in the Virginia school system.

Richmond is rich in remembrances of times past. Richmond National Battlefield Park includes important sites associated with Union attempts to capture the Confederate capital during the Civil War. (The battlefield park is treated in detail in Tour IV.) Virginia Union University, established after the Civil War, is considered one of the outstanding predominantly black schools in the United States. For maps of the city and travel hints, stop at one of the Richmond Visitor Centers: downtown in 6th Street Market Place, Main Street Station, and at Exit 14 off Routes I-95/64.

Booker T. Washington was born April 5, 1856, into slavery, as the son of Jane Ferguson a slave-cook on a small farm in Franklin County, Virginia.

"Up From Slavery"

Such is the title of the autobiography of Booker T. Washington, who was born in 1856 on a small Franklin County plantation in the foothills of the Blue Ridge Mountains about 20 miles southeast of Roanoke, VA. It was a time when state law prohibited him or any slave from attending school or learning to read. Booker T. Washington National Monument shows what life was like, how slaveowner and slave worked to raise tobacco and subsistence crops, and how one small boy dreamed of overcoming all odds to achieve a worthwhile career. As a child he had no last name; he later chose "Washington."

Of Men and Women Who Inspired the Nation

"My life had its beginning in the midst of the most miserable, desolate and discouraging surroundings," Booker T. Washington wrote many years later. "In my childhood I had suffered for want of a place to sleep, for lack of food, clothing, and shelter." The restored 19th century farm embraces buildings, tools, crops, animals and, at times, people in the dress of the period of which he wrote. The Plantation Trail, starting from the visitor center, reveals many aspects of plantation life. Visiting Booker's earliest home—a reconstructed kitchen cabin with dirt floor and no glass windows—demonstrates the challenges he faced to become an eminent educator, presidential adviser and leader of black Americans.

When freedom came at the end of the Civil War, Booker T. Washington left the plantation to work in a salt furnace and coal mine. Life was still harsh, but reading was allowed. With the encouragement of his mother, he taught himself the alphabet and never ceased striving to improve. In due course he would write, "From the time I can remember having any thoughts about anything, I had an intense longing to learn to read."

Booker Washington went on to establish Tuskegee Institute in Alabama to provide practical training to black Americans so they could achieve economic independence. He became the acknowledged spokesman of his race, honored by Harvard University, consulted by the White House, and widely respected at home and abroad. By the time of his death in 1915, he had traveled a long road from the old Burroughs Plantation.

Yet the barns, sheds, pastures, crops, and farm animals tell the story of the beginning—of the yearning, determination and self-assigned responsi-

A kitchen cabin, similar to this reconstructed small log cabin with a dirt floor, doubled as home for Booker, and his mother, brother and sister.

bility. "It is important and right that all privileges of the law be ours, but it is vastly more important that we be prepared for the exercise of those privileges," Washington declared in an 1895 speech, and he might well have been speaking to people everywhere, of all races, and of all times.

Travel tips and tidbits

Booker T. Washington National Monument is an easy side trip from the Blue Ridge Parkway. From Roanoke drive to Rocky Mount, then 11 miles northeast. The national monument includes a picnic area, but you'll find much more extensive facilities at nearby Smith Mountain Lake State Park, and south of Rocky Mount at Fairy Stone State Park (including tent and trailer sites, swimming beach, and hiking trails).

Points of interest in tracing the road up from slavery include: Malden, just east of Charleston, WV, where Booker learned the alphabet and chose a second name; Hampton Institute, Hampton, VA, where he was graduated in 1875; and Tuskegee Institute, at Tuskegee AL, which he founded in 1881 with 30 students, two rundown buildings, and $2,000 for salaries. Tuskegee Institute National Historic Site now includes his home—the Oaks—restored to its early 20th century appearance. The school has expanded to 161 buildings with 3,500 students.

Albert Gallatin, 1761-1849. Portrait by Gilbert Stuart, immigrated from Switzerland in 1780, later becoming a statesman, financier and diplomat for the young American republic.

If You're Coming from the West—

Nestled on a scenic plateau of the Laurel Mountains in southwestern Pennsylvania, Friendship Hill National Historic Site preserves the country estate and recounts the life of Albert Gallatin. He was a man of extraordinary

131

talent, who figured prominently in the early history of the United States. He was an immigrant from Switzerland, who made significant contributions to our young republic over a span of 70 years.

Gallatin is best remembered as Secretary of the Treasury under Presidents Jefferson and Madison and for his concept of the first National Road (today's U.S.Route 40). He also served as chief negotiator of the treaty ending the War of 1812 and as United States envoy to both France and Britain. He was a frontier pioneer in his own right, building Friendship Hill in 1789. The house still stands on the banks of Monongahela River.

The house, made of local stone and shaded by fine old trees, is currently undergoing restoration. While this is going on, park rangers lead visitors

By 1790, Gallatin had purchased land in western Pennsylvania, had begun a new settlement named New Geneva, and added to his farm home, Friendship Hill.

on tours of the house, pointing out various architectural details being discovered during the restoration.

A great deal about Gallatin and his talents can be learned from a visit here. He received an excellent education in Switzerland, but his interest in radical ideas—such as Rousseau's call for a return to nature—led to a break with his family and an abrupt departure for America shortly before he was 19. He tried unsuccessfully, for a time, to sell West Indian merchandise to Maine farmers, and then later taught French at Harvard.

In 1784, caught up in the spirit of the new country, he set out across the Alleghenies with a small exploring party. These early adventures were a prelude to his career in public service, which included several terms as a member of Congress before becoming a cabinet member and diplomat. But there was even more to his career. During his later years, he was president of the National Bank of New York, helped found New York University, and founded the American Ethnological Society of New York, thus earning the title of "Father of American Ethnology."

Be sure to walk the loop trail around the beautiful grounds surrounding the house. It is particularly attractive during spring wildflower and fall foliage seasons. Five miles of trails provide a closeup of woods, meadows, and streams.

Travel tips and tidbits

Friendship Hill is four miles north of Point Marion, PA, midway between Uniontown and Morgantown, WV. It makes a pleasant stop if you're heading for a rafting trip on the Cheat, New or Gauley Rivers in West Virginia.

Fort Necessity National Battlefield, PA, the scene of George Washington's first major battle as an "Englishman" fighting the French (treated in detail in Tour I) is only 25 miles away. Mount Washington Tavern, overlooking the fort, was built on the National Road (now U.S. 40), which Gallatin conceived as a gateway to the West. As Jefferson's Secretary of the Treasury, he encouraged the Lewis and Clark expedition to the Pacific; the Gallatin River in Montana was named for him.

Special events at Friendship Hill include: Blooming Days Wildflower Walks on April weekends; Restoration Day in **May,** *highlighting the restoration of the house; Children's Nature Walk, with special activities for children under 12, in* **mid-July***; U.S. Constitution Day, marking Western Pennsylvania's role in shaping the Constitution, on the* **Sunday closest to September 17***; and FestiFall, with traditional Allegheny arts and crafts,* **the first Sunday in October.**

When at the farm as President, Eisenhower displayed the Presidential standard and U.S. flag; when reinstated as General of the Army, he flew the five-star flag.

Ike and Mamie—Living with History Leaving it for Others

Dwight and Mamie Eisenhower had lived in almost 40 places in their lives together, yet never owned a home of their own until the farm at Gettysburg. Now that they are gone, the house and grounds are carefully preserved to appear as in their time. To maintain the tranquil appearance, the number of visitors is limited. Access is by a shuttle bus from the visitor center at nearby Gettysburg National Military Park where tickets are distributed on a first come first served basis for each day's scheduled tours of the farm. It may take a little time and effort, but you'll enjoy it.

Dwight D. Eisenhower loved Gettysburg. Though born in Texas and raised in Kansas, he served during World War I at an Army post in Gettysburg, about 50 miles south of his ancestors' settlement. In 1950, while president of Columbia University, the Eisenhowers looked for a permanent home and found one at Gettysburg.

The Eisenhower farm home served as a retreat during their Presidential years, and then as their residence and retirement home.

Ike wrote in his 1967 autobiography, "Mamie ....wanted a place that conformed to her notions of what a home should be."

But they would not settle down there for some years. From Columbia, Eisenhower became commander of North Atlantic Treaty Organization forces in Europe. Then in 1952, he was elected to succeed his commander-in-chief, Harry S. Truman, and became 34th President of the United States. Although the Eisenhowers used their farm as a "weekend White House," their official resident was the White House in Washington, DC. Finally in 1961, following his second term as President, the Eisenhowers retired to their Gettysburg home.

The Eisenhower farm adjoins Gettysburg National Military Park and enhances the pastoral environs. Eisenhower often said he wanted to "leave the place better than I found it." But leave it to whom and for what purpose? In 1967, Ike and Mamie made a gift of the property to the people of the United States, reserving the right of lifetime occupancy. He died in 1969 and she ten years later. The house has been open to the public since 1980.

The "modified Georgian farmhouse" is furnished much as when the former First Family occupied it, including the furniture and decorative objects Mamie had collected for years, and the original paintings by Dwight Eisenhower. "Mamie, who had spent a lifetime adjusting herself to other people's housing designs," wrote Ike in his 1967 autobiography, "wanted a place that conformed to her notions of what a home should be." It is plainly, both a home for comfort and a showplace for entertaining dignitaries and heads of state, including Nikita Krushchev, Charles DeGaulle, and Winston Churchill.

Beginning at the Reception Center (once a Secret Service office), a self-guiding walking tour leads to various points of interest, such as the Norway spruce trees lining the driveway, 1955 birthday presents from Republican state chairmen; the putting green, presented by the Professional Golfers Association; the brass "Frisco Bell," the gift of a railway company; and the garage, once a chicken house, housing the modern "Surrey with the Fringe on Top," which the Eisenhowers used to tour guests around the farm.

Travel tips and tidbits

To be certain you get to visit the Eisenhower Farm, stop early at the National Park Service Visitor Center—especially during summer or a peak weekend. The visitor center opens at 8 a.m. (The Gettysburg battlefield is covered in detail in Tour IV.)

For a pleasant side trip, drive north to Carlisle and visit Carlisle Barracks, one of the oldest military posts in the country. It includes the Omar Bradley Museum, containing personal items of the five-star general who served with Eisenhower. Stop at Pine Grove Furnace State Park, the site of a pre-Revolutionary iron forge where facilities include tent and trailer camping, picnicking, hiking, and swimming.

Principal Eisenhower sites elsewhere in the country are Eisenhower Birthplace State Historic Site, at Denison, TX, restored to its appearance at the time of his birth in 1890; and the Eisenhower Center, at Abilene, KS, which includes his boyhood home, the Eisenhower Library with his presidential papers, and the Meditation Chapel, where Dwight and Mamie Eisenhower are buried.

Clara Barton devoted her life to helping soldiers on the battlefields as well as civilians caught in natural disasters. Her home reflects her resourcefulness and dedication.

The Professional Angel

"You must never so much as think whether you like it or not, whether it is bearable or not; you must never think anything except the need, and how to meet it." Clara Barton, 1866. In Glen Echo, MD, a suburb of Washington DC, the Clara Barton National Historic Site memorializes the life of this woman who established the American branch of the Red Cross.

Here you can see many of her personal effects and some of the awards given her for her work—her nursing on the battlefields of the U.S. Civil War, her formation of a bureau to track missing soldiers, her nursing during the Russian and Armenian famine, her relief efforts at the Johnstown flood of 1889, and later after the flood in Galveston, TX.

Clara Barton was born on Christmas Day in 1821, on a farm in Oxford, MA. In 1854 she became the first female clerk in the patent office. At that time she was the only female employee of the government! In 1891 she built this house, warehouse, and headquarters of the American branch of the Red Cross, from the lumber salvaged from the temporary housing used at Johnstown. She became the first president of the American branch of the Red Cross in 1882 and held that post until 1904.

Strongly supporting women's equality, she believed in their right to vote. She wrote several books and took active parts in many kinds of charitable and patriotic work. For this she was awarded 10 badges and medals from foreign countries. She died on April 12, 1912, at the age of 90.

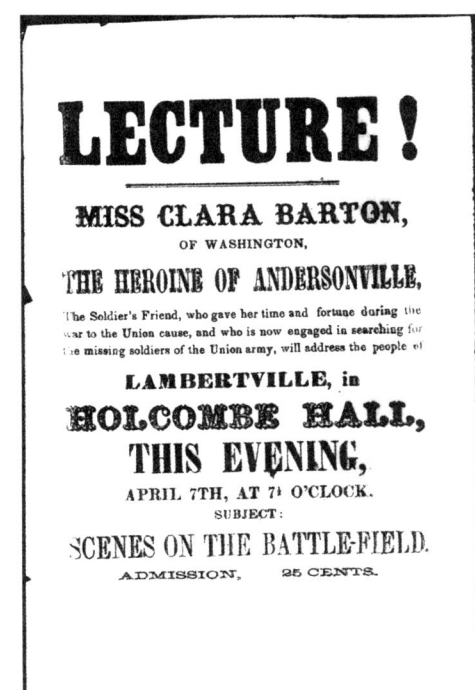

Despite bouts of nervousness Clara Barton enjoyed public speaking and was in great demand as a lecturer, talking either about her Civil War experiences or woman's rights.

Park Information

Booker T. Washington National Monument
RT 1, Box 195
Hardy, VA 24101
(703) 721-2094

Visitor Center—From Roanoke, VA go 12 miles south on State Rt. 116 to Burnt Chimney then 4 miles east on State Rt. 122 (this is also the closest accest from the Blue Ridge Parkway). From Bedford, VA go south 23 miles on State Rt. 122.

Visitor Center hours 9:00—5:00

Clara Barton National Historic Site
5801 Oxford Road
Glen Echo, MD 20812
(301) 492-6245

Visitor Center—Take Interstate 495 to the Glen Echo exit—you will be traveling East, follow the signs to Glen Echo and a National Park Service sign, make a left at the NPS sign; you will see a large parking lot with signs directing you to the Clara Barton house.

Visitor Center hours 8:30—5:00, 7 days a week (Closed all Federal Holidays). *All tours are guided, the last tour begins at 4:30 pm.
*For groups of ten (10) or more, reservations are required.

Edison National Historic Site
Main Street and Lakeside Avenue
West Orange, NJ 07052
Information (201) 736-5050
Reservations (201) 736-1515

Visitor Center—The Edison Laboratories are located on Main St. in West Orange, a short distance from Route I-280. When traveling East on I-280, take Exit #9; when traveling West take Exit #10. Signs from both exits mark the one-mile route to the Edison Laboratories. The visitor center entrance is located around the corner from the parking lot on Lakeside Avenue.

Visitor Center hours 9:00—5:00 daily. Tours available Wednesday thru Sunday (last tour at 3:30 pm)

Edgar Allan Poe National Historic Site
Independence National Historical Park
313 Walnut Street
Philadelphia, PA 19106
(215) 597-8780

Visitor Center—7th & Spring Garden Streets.

Visitor Center hours 9:00—5:00 daily

Eisenhower National Historic Site
Taneytown Road
Gettysburg, PA 17325
(717) 334-1124

Visitor Center—One mile south of Gettysburg town square on Business Route 15. From Washington (the south), take Business 15 (Steinwehr Avenue exit) off 15. Visitor center will be on right as you enter town. From east, west, or north, go to town square and take Baltimore Street south. At second light, bear right. Visitor Center will be on left two blocks ahead.

Visitor Center hours 8:30—4:30 daily April—October. Closed Monday and Tuesday November—March. Closed Thanksgiving, Christmas, and New Years Day, and closed four weeks beginning the first Sunday following New Years Day.

Franklin Court
Independence National Historical Park
313 Walnut Street
Philadelphia, PA 19106
(215) 597-8974 or 75

Visitor Center—Each of the following sets of directions will lead you to the parking garage on 2d Street between Chestnut and Walnut Streets. Eastbound via I-76 (Schuylkill Expressway): Exit at Vine Street (I-676 and U.S. 30) and follow to 6th Street. Turn right on 6th and follow to Chestnut (3 blocks). Turn left on Chestnut and follow to 2d Street. Turn right on 2d street. **Westbound** via Benjamin Franklin Bridge (U.S. 30): As you come off the bridge, follow the signs to 6th Street (south). From there, follow the same directions as outlined for Eastbound to reach 2d Street.

Of Men and Women Who Inspired the Nation

Southbound via I-95: Take the Center City exit to 2d Street. **Northbound** via I-95: Exit at Taster Street. Continue straight ahead to Reed Street. Turn right on Reed and follow to Delaware Avenue. Turn left on Delaware Avenue and follow to the exit for Market Street (on right). When you reach Market, make an immediate left onto 2d Street.

Visitor Center hours 9:00—5:00 (Sept.-June); 9:00—6:00 (July-August).

Friendship Hill National Historic Site
c/o Fort Necessity National Park
RD 2, Box 528
Farmington, PA 15437
(412) 725-9190

Visitor Center—4 miles north of Point Marion, PA along PA Route 166; approximately midway between Uniontown, PA and Morgantown, WV.

Visitor Center hours 9:30—5:00; Daily: Memorial Day—Labor Day. Weekends only rest of year.

George Washington Birthplace National Monument
RR 1, Box 717
Washington's Birthplace, VA 22575
(804) 224-1732

Visitor Center—38 miles east of Fredericksburg, VA via Route 3. Turn left on Route 204 approximately 2 miles.

Visitor Center hours 9:00—5:00

Maggie L. Walker National Historic Site
110½ East Leigh Street
Richmond, VA 23219
(804) 780-1380

Visitor Center—The Maggie L. Walker House is located at the intersection of 2d and East Leigh Street in downtown Richmond. Access may be gained via 2d Street North (one-way) or from East Leigh Street which is an East-West artery. From I-95 South take the 3rd Street exit to East Leigh and turn right to 2d Street.

Visitor Center hours 9:00—5:00 Thurs., Fri., Sat. & Sun.

Designed and Produced By:
Rich Timmons and Associates, Furlong, PA

Editing and Photographic Selection:
Division of Interpretation and Visitor Service
Mid-Atlantic Region, National Park Service
Chet Harris, Lea Murray and Mid-Atlantic Parks' Staff

Word Processing:
Patricia Glass, Marcella Brinkley

Photography Credits:
All from the collections of the United States Department of the Interior
National Park Service
Except for:
p. 28; George Goodwin, Morristown, NJ
pp. 68, 77; Pineland Commission, New Lisbon NJ

Funded by:
A grant from the William Penn Foundation
The Committee to Preserve Assateague
The Friends of the Virginia Civil War Battlefields
The Friends of Independence National Historical Park
The Friends of Valley Forge National Historical Park
Friendship Hill Association

Funds Administered by:
The Friends of Independence National Historical Park